M000289427

in the
INCLUSIVE
SECONDARY
CLASSROOM

WORD STUDY

in the INCLUSIVE SECONDARY CLASSROOM

SUPPORTING STRUGGLING READERS & STUDENTS WITH DISABILITIES

Melinda M. Leko

TEACHERS COLLEGE PRESS

TEACHERS COLLEGE | COLUMBIA UNIVERSITY

NEW YORK AND LONDON

Published by Teachers College Press, 1234 Amsterdam Avenue, New York, NY 10027

Copyright © 2016 by Teachers College, Columbia University

Cover design by Holly Grundon/BHG Graphic Design

All rights reserved. No part of this publication may be reproduced or transmitted in any form or by any means, electronic or mechanical, including photocopy, or any information storage and retrieval system, without permission from the publisher.

Library of Congress Cataloging-in-Publication Data

Names: Leko, Melinda M.
    Title: Word study in the inclusive secondary classroom : Supporting struggling readers and students with disabilities / Melinda M. Leko.
Description: New York, NY : Teachers College Press, 2016. | Includes bibliographical references and index.
Identifiers: LCCN 2016005848| ISBN 9780807757789 (pbk. : alk. paper) | ISBN 9780807757796 (hardcover : alk. paper)
Subjects: LCSH: Vocabulary—Study and teaching (Secondary) | Word study-- Study and teaching (Secondary) | Inclusive education.
Classification: LCC LB1631 .L348 2016 | DDC 428.10712—dc23
LC record available at http://lccn.loc.gov/2016005848

ISBN 978-0-8077-5778-9 (paper)
ISBN 978-0-8077-5779-6 (hardcover)
ISBN 978-0-8077-7487-8 (ebook)

Printed on acid-free paper
Manufactured in the United States of America

23 22 21 20 19 18 17 16   8 7 6 5 4 3 2 1

To Adam, MaryAnne, and Ella

Contents

Acknowledgments

This book would not have been possible without the support of the outstanding team at Teachers College Press. In particular I would like to thank Emily Spangler for inspiring and encouraging me throughout the entire process. I am especially grateful for the amazing feedback Emily provided on earlier drafts of this book. I know the book has been made stronger due to her exemplary skills as an editor.

I am indebted to my advisor, Dr. Mary Brownell, who has been a constant source of support since day one of my doctoral program. She has instilled in me the confidence to take on new challenges, grow as a researcher, and tackle the really hard questions. I am incredibly honored to call her a mentor, colleague, and friend. I am also thankful for the support of my wide network of formal and informal mentors at the University of Florida, the University of Wisconsin–Madison, and the University of Kansas, including Paul Sindelar, Cynthia Griffin, Kimber Wilkerson, Audrey Trainor, Kathleen Lane, and Karrie Shogren. I am also appreciative of all of my colleagues within the fields of reading, special education, and teacher education, whose research and service continue to improve outcomes for students with disabilities and their families.

Finally, this book would not be possible without the love and support of my wonderful family. To my daughters, MaryAnne and Ella, thank you for keeping me young at heart and reminding me of the magic of reading. I am so grateful to my parents, Wayne and Judy Cothern, and my sisters, Debbie and Melissa, for being my first and very best teachers. I also thank my mother- and father-in-law, Janet and Dave Leko, and my brother- and sisters-in-law, Melissa, Kevin, Chris, and Ashley, for always being there for me. Finally, my unending appreciation goes to my husband, Adam. It is because of his support, humor, and love that this book came to fruition.

Introduction

The focus of *Word Study in the Inclusive Secondary Classroom* is on providing effective and efficient word study instruction in inclusive secondary classrooms. Word study is the combination of phonics, spelling, and vocabulary instruction. In word study, students are taught to examine words based on their parts and patterns, thereby improving students' ability to decode unknown words, determine their meaning, and spell them independently.

Why devote an entire book to word study at the secondary level (i.e., both middle and high school)? The answer is that word study instruction can help struggling readers and students with disabilities succeed in general education content area classrooms. Specifically, word study instruction can help struggling readers and students with disabilities break apart long, complex, and often unfamiliar words commonly found in challenging content area texts.

In this book I often refer to "students with disabilities." Generally speaking I am referring to students who have been formally identified as having a reading disability. A reading disability is a type of specific learning disability. According to the Individuals with Disabilities Education Act (IDEA; 2004):

> the term "specific learning disability" means a disorder in one or more of the basic psychological processes involved in understanding or in using language, spoken or written, which disorder may manifest itself in imperfect ability to listen, think, speak, read, write, spell, or do mathematical calculations.

Under IDEA (2004), "students are eligible for special education services for a specific learning disability in reading (i.e., reading disability) if: (a) there exists a severe discrepancy between students' potential learning ability (usually measured by an IQ score) and their reading achievement, or (b) students fail to respond to research-based interventions, a process known as Response-to-Intervention (RTI)" (Leko, Mundy, & Kiely, 2009, p. 6). It is important to note, however, that students identified with other disability types (e.g., attention-deficit/ hyperactivity disorder [ADHD], emotional and behavioral disorders [EBD]) may also struggle in reading, a discussion addressed more fully in Chapter 2.

Alternatively, not all students who struggle with reading have disabilities. Clear inequalities have emerged in reading proficiency along racial, cultural, linguistic, and economic lines, often referred to as the achievement or opportunity gap. For example, 71% of English language learners (ELLs), 42% of Black students, and 34% of Hispanic students read below basic level in 8th grade according to the National Assessment of Educational Progress (NAEP; U.S. Department of Education, 2015). Statistics on the reading achievement of students with disabilities are similarly disconcerting. Approximately 63% of 8th- and 12th-grade students with disabilities read below basic level (U.S. Department of Education, 2015). Part of the solution to the achievement gap is secondary teachers being actively involved in supporting students' reading achievement, and word study is a logical and beneficial place to start.

Why do so many students enter middle and high school with such poor reading skills? It is in part because after 4th grade most students do not receive explicit reading instruction. If students struggle with reading at the end of elementary school, it is difficult for them to ever catch up to their peers unless they receive targeted support in reading within each of their classes. Take, for example, students with learning disabilities (LD) and emotional and behavioral disorders (EBD). Approximately 80% of students with learning disabilities and 75% of students with emotional and behavioral disabilities take one or more academic general education classes (Newman, 2006; Wagner & Cameto, 2004). When enrolled in these courses, these students are expected to keep up with their peers without disabilities. Teachers report, however, that more than 25% of students with LD and 33% of students with EBD are not able to do so (Wagner & Cameto, 2004). Similar patterns exist for English language learners and other students of diverse backgrounds (Klingner, Artiles, & Barletta, 2006; Reeves, 2006). These troubling findings can be explained, in part, by students' difficulties reading challenging content area texts and by teachers in content area classes not being prepared to teach reading and/or not believing that teaching reading is their priority (Greenleaf, Schoenbach, Cziko, & Mueller, 2001; Kamil, 2003).

The good news is that adolescence is not too late to intervene (Scammacca et al., 2007). Older students, both with and without learning disabilities, benefit from targeted interventions at both the word and text level. When providing such interventions, experts recommend they be couched in content area materials and texts (Biancarosa & Snow, 2006; Faggella-Luby, Ware, & Capozzoli, 2009). This is where learning how to provide word study instruction in secondary general education classrooms comes into play—instruction that can benefit many students.

Take a look at the following sentences from middle and high school curricular materials:

- "As the Roman Empire collapsed in the fifth century, more and more people fled to the countryside to escape invaders from the north and east" (Holt McDougal, *World Cultures and Geography Eastern Hemisphere,* p. 84).
- "Both the constant term and the leading coefficient of a polynomial can play a role in identifying the rational roots of the related polynomial equation" (Prentice Hall, *Algebra 2,* p. 329).
- "At transform boundaries, two plates slide past one another without converging or diverging" (McGraw-Hill, *Earth Materials and Processes,* p. 114).

The sentences above would likely pose difficulties for many struggling readers and students with disabilities for a number of reasons. Sentences like these that are often found in secondary texts contain complex multisyllabic words, sophisticated text structures, and discipline-specific vocabulary (Barton, Heidema, & Jordan, 2002; Kenney, Hancewicz, Heuer, Metsisto, & Tuttle, 2005). Students might not have sufficient background knowledge of the subject matter, so the vocabulary and concepts will be unfamiliar. Moreover, the texts may be written on reading levels higher than struggling readers and students with disabilities can successfully read independently (Barton et al., 2002). Finally, in the case of English language learners, exceptions to regular American English decoding and spelling patterns, advanced academic vocabulary, and differences in letter-sound correspondences across languages can make reading and understanding secondary texts challenging (Linan-Thompson & Vaughn, 2007).

Although the focus of this book is on improving the reading success of struggling readers and students with disabilities, teachers may find that the information and strategies distilled in this book can help their other students as well. All students can benefit from strategies that help them independently determine the meaning of novel vocabulary words, particularly as some estimates indicate college-bound students should have between 75,000 and 120,000 words in their vocabularies by 12th grade (Heller, 2015). Moreover, with many states adopting the Common Core State Standards (CCSS), it is critical for secondary teachers to have more preparation in the area of literacy. The CCSS are a set of academic standards in English/language arts and mathematics that provide guidance on what students should know and be able to do at the end of each grade in order to graduate college and be career ready (Common Core State Standards Initiative [CCSSI], n.d.). The CCSS have ratcheted up expectations for students and teachers by placing greater emphasis on literacy instruction within content areas. The CCSS requires instruction that helps students acquire skills to read, write, speak, listen, and reason within and across disciplines (CCSSI, n.d.). The CCSS also promote students' acquisition of academic language and the building of knowledge within disciplines through reading and writing (CCSSI, n.d.). In essence, for students to be able to read, write, speak, listen, and reason successfully across disciplines, they will need greater facility with the words used within specific content areas. In this way, word study can be an important ally for secondary teachers.

My hope is that the information and strategies presented in this book will support teachers and students as they strive to attain the heightened CCSS literacy expectations within the content areas. Having strategies to decode and understand complex multisyllabic words contained in secondary content area texts will make texts more accessible to struggling readers and students with disabilities. With greater awareness of letter–sound correspondences and origins of American English words, students should also find writing within the content areas easier.

The purpose of this book is not to transform every secondary teacher into a reading specialist or expert. In fact, older struggling readers and students with disabilities will need extended, intensive, individualized, and evidence-based reading intervention delivered by highly trained and skilled specialists (O'Connor, 2007). Implementation of the strategies presented in this book, therefore, does not supplant the need for intensive intervention for some students. The key to supporting students' reading achievement and success in general education classrooms is a combined effort between reading specialists and general education teachers. Reading specialists can provide intensive interventions that address individual students' specific areas of need in reading generally, while general education teachers can provide word study instruction and strategies that align with specific content areas. This type of joint effort between reading specialists and general education teachers results in students being provided with reading support throughout their entire school day—a necessary factor in students with disabilities and struggling readers making progress in reading.

This book introduces foundational knowledge and practical strategies so all secondary teachers can embed word study in their daily instruction. Once students have learned the up-front, basic strategies, incorporating word study instruction in content area classrooms takes minimal class time and can actually become a natural part of instruction. Word study instruction will mean struggling readers and students with disabilities will have more tools with which to decode and understand multisyllabic words found in content area texts. This book encourages all secondary teachers both to be familiar with the typical difficulties struggling readers and students with disabilities experience in reading and also to implement simple, yet effective, strategies and interventions in classrooms to address students' reading needs in the areas of decoding, spelling, and vocabulary.

The book is divided into three sections. "Part I: The Whats, Hows, and Whys of Reading for Struggling Readers and Students with Disabilities" provides foundational knowledge about the reading process (Chapter 1), why some students struggle with reading (Chapter 2), and the nature of American English (Chapter 3). "Part II: The Nuts and Bolts of Word Study" provides information on getting started including word study instruction in secondary classrooms (Chapter 4) and word study methods and strategies (Chapter 5). "Part III: Word Study in Secondary Classrooms" situates knowledge and strategies from the first two sections in secondary content area classrooms (Chapter 6) and provides practical tips and tricks for making word study instruction a natural part of instruction (Chapter 7).

Each chapter includes questions for discussion. Chapters also include "Tech Tips," which provide resources for incorporating technology-based and multimedia instruction, as well as other online resources. In several chapters I present classroom vignettes with hypothetical students and teachers that represent trends I have seen in middle and high school classrooms as a way of providing a concrete picture of how to incorporate the book's content seamlessly into a variety of classroom contexts. The appendix provides additional resources that can assist secondary teachers in implementing the ideas presented in the book, some of which can be found online at www.tcpress.com.

Part I

THE WHATS, HOWS, AND WHYS OF READING FOR STRUGGLING READERS AND STUDENTS WITH DISABILITIES

CHAPTER I

The Reading Process

When implementing word study instruction, it is helpful to have a basic understanding of the reading process and how the elements of word study (i.e., decoding, spelling, and vocabulary) are interrelated. With such an understanding teachers can maximize instructional effectiveness by more accurately identifying student decoding and spelling errors and then crafting instruction that directly addresses those errors. Furthermore, by understanding the relationship between decoding, spelling, and vocabulary, teachers can increase word study instructional efficiency so that lessons in decoding can also address spelling and/or vocabulary knowledge and vice versa. This information is also critical when implementing and interpreting assessment data to pinpoint student strengths and weaknesses in reading (more on assessment in Chapter 4).

Reading is a complex skill. The goal of reading is comprehension of text, but to achieve this goal is no small feat! Proficient reading is dependent on several automated mental processes operating concurrently (Adams, 1990; Ehri & Snowling, 2004). First, readers must visually process the symbols on the printed page. As readers' eyes focus on the sequences of letters, several knowledge bases and cognitive processes are stimulated (Ehri & Snowling, 2004). Readers draw on lexical knowledge, or knowledge about specific words and their spellings. Readers also draw on knowledge about the writing system and its conventions. Finally, readers rely on phonological knowledge, or knowledge of sound patterns (O'Connor, 2007).

As readers recognize the various combinations of letters as specific words, they draw on their syntactic knowledge of grammatical relations and their semantic knowledge of word meanings (Ehri & Snowling, 2004). As successive words are put together, readers process them in the form of sentences. When reading sentences, readers must update their memory of previous text and integrate new information, all the while focusing attention on comprehension processes (Ehri & Snowling, 2004; Honig, Diamond, & Gutlohn, 2000).

RELATIONSHIPS BETWEEN READERS, CONTEXTS, AND TEXTS

The reading process and whether it occurs successfully is dependent on several relationships between readers, contexts, and texts. In essence, individual traits of readers, the contexts in which they read, and the actual texts they read interact to either facilitate or hinder the reading process. Of particular importance is readers' incoming background knowledge, motivation, and attention for reading a particular text.

Background Knowledge

The reading process is easier when readers have background knowledge on the text they are reading. For example, read the following two passages:

1. But there's really a lot more to sail trim than just the sheet—there's halyard tension, outhaul tension, traveler adjustment, boom vang tension, and so on. Sometimes it's better if the top of the sail twists relative to the bottom, to spill wind on a blustery day; do this by pulling the traveler in and easing the sheet to let the boom lift in hard puffs of wind. But on a calm day the sail should have little twist, which means increasing sheet tension and adjusting in-or-out position with the traveler.
2. There's no ground impact when you swim, and so you protect the joints from stress and strain. In fact, the Arthritis Foundation strongly recommends swimming and water activities for this reason, so much so that they sponsor water classes all over the country. There's nothing like it during the hot days of summer, whether it's at the beach or in the pool. It's relaxing, the movements are smooth and rhythmic, and it's a great workout.

For many people, the first passage is more difficult to read. It comes from an article about learning the basics of sailing (Discover Boating, 2015). Unless you are an experienced sailor, your limited background knowledge of the topic, including pertinent vocabulary, makes comprehending the passage difficult. Lack of background knowledge about sailing means readers cannot readily create visual images of what is being communicated.

The second passage, which discusses the benefits of swimming (Weil, 2015), is probably a more familiar topic for many readers. Greater background knowledge results in readers having more familiarity with vocabulary and concepts relevant to the topic. It also means readers have more mental "hooks" upon which to hang new information. Readers familiar with swimming can recall times when they have gone swimming and can more easily relate to the author's argument that swimming is easy on the body's joints.

Whenever I think of the power of background knowledge, I am reminded of the years I taught in Florida. I vividly remember my native Floridian students having difficulty comprehending a text about living in the snowy north. Phrases like "snow plow" and "salting the roads" were completely unknown to students who grew up in a state that can be best described as having two seasons: hot and very hot!

Purpose, Motivation, and Attention

Readers read different texts for different purposes. Some texts are meant to promote leisure and enjoyment. Other texts are informational or persuasive. The purpose for reading a particular text can impact readers' motivation and attention. For example, the latest mystery novel by my favorite fiction author is something I want to read. I am motivated to read the novel, and it keeps my attention. I can read it quickly and understand it easily. Purpose, motivation, and attention interact in positive ways to promote the reading process.

On the other hand, having to read an article about how to install new mandatory software updates on my laptop is not something I want to read. It is something I am forced to read if I want a properly functioning computer. As a tech-laggard, I lack background knowledge and familiarity with technical terms like DMG file, disk image, installer PKG files, and patches. When trying to read this text my attention is likely to wander, and I may have to read it several times before fully comprehending it. In this situation, purpose, motivation, and attention interact to make the reading process more difficult.

READING INSTRUCTION: FIVE AREAS OF READING

For many students, learning to read is a smooth process and occurs successfully without significant interventions. However, this is not the case for a concerning percentage of students. Data from the National Assessment of Educational Progress provides information on the reading achievement of students in grades 4, 8, and 12 (NAEP; U.S. Department of Education, 2015). Approximately 71% of English language learners, 42% of Black students, 34% of Hispanic students, and 63% of students with disabilities read below basic level in 8th grade (NAEP;

U.S. Department of Education, 2015). These statistics bring up issues of equity, and, as I discuss in Chapter 2, differences in students' linguistic, racial, cultural, and economic backgrounds play a large role in students' reading achievement and experiences with reading instruction throughout school. Incorporating word study instruction in secondary classrooms is one way to help decrease the achievement gap between distinct groups of students and explicitly provide support to students who struggle in reading for any number of reasons.

In response to mounting concerns about students' poor achievement in reading, researchers and policymakers invested considerable time and resources to answer the question: What is effective reading instruction? The answer is that effective reading instruction is comprised of systematic and explicit instruction in five areas: phonemic awareness, phonics, fluency, vocabulary, and comprehension (National Reading Panel [NRP], 2000). Proficiency in each of these areas is necessary for students to be successful readers, and each area of reading is related to the others. So although this book focuses specifically on the areas of reading that comprise word study, it is helpful to be familiar with the other areas of reading and how they influence student's acquisition of word study skills and strategies.

Phonemic Awareness

Phonemic awareness "is the ability to notice, think about, and work with the individual sounds in spoken words" (Armbruster et al., 2003, p. 2). The individual sounds in words are formally referred to as *phonemes*. An example of instruction in phonemic awareness might involve asking a student to identify the initial sound in the word *cat*.

Phonemic awareness is an important foundational reading skill. It paves the way for students to successfully pair letter sounds with printed letters. Phonemic awareness helps students understand that there are predictable and systematic relationships between printed letters and letter sounds—a concept called the "alphabetic principle."

An important fact to keep in mind is that phonemic awareness is a completely auditory skill. Phonemic awareness is the manipulation of sounds, not printed letters. It is all based on what is said and heard. Close your eyes and say the sounds in the word *cat*. See? Phonemic awareness activities can be done in the dark.

Phonemic awareness is made up of several skills that increase in complexity. Figure 1.1 illustrates the progression of phonemic awareness skills with examples.

"If books are food for the mind, then this one
needs salt, ketchup, mustard, and a side of fries!"

Figure 1.1. Phonemic Awareness Skills

Discriminating & Identifying	Blending	Segmenting	Deleting & Adding	Substituting
• What is the first sound in *boat*? • What sound is the same in *map, mud,* and *milk*?	• What word does /k/ /i/ /t/ make?	• What are the sounds in *step*?	• What word do you get when you add /s/ to the word *top*?	• The word is *bet*. Change the /t/ to a /d/. What is the new word?

Simple to Complex

The most basic skills are discriminating and identifying phonemes. An example would be asking students to identify the number of phonemes in the word *step*. After discriminating and identifying comes blending. This is when students are asked to say full words after hearing the individual phonemes. An example would be asking students to say the word that the sounds /f/ /a/ /n/ make. The opposite of blending is segmenting. This is when students are asked to break apart words into their individual phonemes. *Map* would be /m/ /a/ /p/. The next skill is deleting and adding phonemes. Students could be asked to add or delete a phoneme from the beginning or end of words. Asking students what word is made when /b/ is added to the word *lock* is an example. Finally, the most complex phonemic awareness skill is substitution, in which one phoneme is replaced with a different one. For example, students could be asked to change the /p/ sound in *pin* with the /t/ sound to make *tin*.

Phonics

Phonics is the connection between letter sounds (phonemes) and printed letters (graphemes) (Lane, Pullen, Eisle, & Jordan, 2005; NRP, 2000). When students use their knowledge of the alphabetic principle, they are able to read or decode new words. If you are able to read the following words: *ket, sluzz, trawing*, it is because you have a well-developed understanding of the alphabetic principle and phonics knowledge. Even though these are nonsense words, you can still decode them by applying phonics conventions.

Extensive research has shown that the best way to teach phonics is to use a systematic and explicit approach (NRP, 2000). This means directly teaching students the relationships between phonemes and graphemes using an instructional scope and sequence that moves from simple to complex. Chapter 3 explores the phonics basics that make up the American English language.

Fluency

Fluency is the ability to read accurately, rapidly, and with expression, or prosody (NRP, 2000; O'Connor & Bell, 2004). When reading aloud, fluent readers sound as if they are speaking or having a conversation.

Fluency is an important link between decoding and comprehension. Fluent readers are able to automatically and accurately decode words, which leaves them with more mental energy to comprehend what they are reading. Nonfluent readers, on the other hand, spend the bulk of their attention decoding words as opposed to comprehending them.

Several instructional practices have been shown to be effective in promoting students' reading fluency. First and foremost is the opportunity for students to read and reread text aloud while receiving feedback on their performance. This can be accomplished by having students read with an adult, read simultaneously in a group (choral reading), repeat or echo when they listen to someone else read, read with a more advanced reader (partner reading), or read aloud with an audiotaped model (tape-assisted reading).

Vocabulary

Vocabulary refers to "the words we must know to communicate effectively" (Armbruster et al., 2003, p. 34). Vocabulary can be broken down into two subtypes: expressive and receptive. *Expressive vocabulary* refers to words used in speaking and writing—the vocabulary we use to express ourselves. Meanwhile, *receptive vocabulary* refers to words used in listening and reading— the words we understand when we receive a message.

Vocabulary knowledge is closely tied to comprehension. Even if students can accurately decode words and fluently read texts, if they do not understand the meaning of key vocabulary, then their comprehension is poor. If a text is all about a *bleb*, but they do not know the meaning of *bleb*, they probably will not understand the text—even if their teacher told them about the time she got a *bleb*. She would have to tell them directly that a *bleb* is a small blister. There are two approaches to vocabulary instruction: direct and indirect. Direct vocabulary instruction makes use of explicit approaches to teach students the meaning of new words and word-learning strategies (Armbruster et al., 2003). Telling students the meaning or definition of *photosynthesis* is an example of direct vocabulary instruction. Indirect vocabulary learning occurs when students acquire the meanings of new words by hearing or seeing them in different contexts. For example, students might indirectly learn the meaning of the word *elated* when their teacher smiles, claps her hands, and says, "I am *elated* that all of you completed your homework last night."

Comprehension

Comprehension simply means understanding what is read. It is the end point in the reading process. It is what results when all of the components of the reading process work in concert. It is not motivating to read a text that you, for whatever reason, cannot comprehend. In fact, without comprehension, what is the point of reading?

Readers with good comprehension skills read with a designated purpose in mind. They actively monitor their own comprehension. When comprehension breaks down, good readers use a variety of strategies to address the problem. Such strategies include:

- **Rereading:** "I didn't quite understand that last paragraph. Let me try reading it again."
- **Looking forward:** "I don't understand what the term *water cycle* means. I am going to flip ahead a few pages to see if there is a diagram or definition."
- **Rephrasing:** "When the author describes the man as being *jovial*, I can tell that she means he is cheerful."
- **Diagnosing cause of comprehension breakdown:** "Why don't I understand? Is it because I read too quickly, or is it because I don't know the meaning of the word *monarch*?"
- **Determining meaning of unknown words:** "Wait. I don't know what the word *evidence* means. I am going to look it up."

Thinking about your own thinking is referred to as *metagcognition* (Garner, 1987; Paris, & Oka, 1986), and the strategies listed above are metacognitive. I can recall times when I was reading and reached the bottom of a page only to realize I had no recollection of what I had just read. Recognizing that I did not comprehend what I had just read is a critical reading skill, one that poor readers often lack. Teaching comprehension means directly teaching metacognitive skills that can repair comprehension breakdowns. It also means teaching students strategies they can use before, during, and after reading to monitor and improve their comprehension.

Summarizing is the process of synthesizing the main ideas from a text. If readers can accurately summarize the main ideas of a text, then they understand what they have read. *Visual imagery* is creating a mental picture of what is read. Having students practice creating visual images of what they read can help them understand and remember the main ideas.

Finally, asking students to answer comprehension questions is a common method for teaching and assessing comprehension. Not all comprehension questions, however, are created equal. Some questions require students to recall basic, factual information (e.g., What did Cinderella lose at the ball?). Other questions require students to comprehend text in more sophisticated ways. Asking students to analyze, synthesize, and evaluate what they read requires more advanced comprehension.

Understanding the five areas of reading and the role they play as part of the reading process is instrumental in assessing and addressing students' reading instructional needs. Such information will help teachers get a better sense of why particular students are struggling with reading in their classes. Perhaps some are able to decode words accurately but read slowly and laboriously. Here is a case in which a student is in need of fluency instruction. For this student, word study instruction will not address an underlying weakness in reading fluency. This is important to know and communicate to a reading teacher or specialist who may be able to provide targeted intervention in fluency. In other cases, however, students might not comprehend text either because they cannot decode difficult words or because they do not know the meanings of words they decode. In these instances word study instruction can come to the rescue.

WORD STUDY

Word study, the focus of this book, is instruction that results from combining phonics (decoding), spelling (encoding), and vocabulary. Word study instruction provides students with tools to decode and spell unknown words, as well as determine word meanings based on word parts. Research has shown that the ability to decode unknown words efficiently and automatically is a trait of skilled readers (Chard, Vaughn, & Tyler, 2002; Rasinski, 2004). Moreover, "the recognition of printed words is the largest barrier in the reading process for children with reading disabilities" (O'Connor, 2007, p. 1). As discussed earlier, word study concepts and strategies can enhance students' success in secondary content area classrooms due to the sheer number of large unfamiliar words students will encounter in content area texts. Word study instruction can help struggling readers and students with disabilities become more independent decoders and word meaning-makers.

In this book I use the term *basic word study* to denote instruction that helps students decode single syllable words, while *advanced word study* refers to instruction that provides students with the necessary skills to tackle more complex, multisyllabic words (see Chapter 5).

READING INSTRUCTION FOR ADOLESCENTS

What about older struggling readers? What instructional approaches work best for them? Research supports direct, explicit vocabulary and comprehension instruction (Biancarosa & Snow, 2006). Recommendations more specific to adolescent readers include embedding reading instruction in content, incorporating diverse texts, including intensive writing instruction, and including text-based collaborative learning (Biancarosa & Snow, 2006). Additional research and policy reports specific to adolescents who have disabilities or who struggle in reading promote interventions at the word and text level, extended discussions of text, and intensive individualized interventions (Kamil et al., 2008; Scammacca et al., 2007).

By understanding the reading process, secondary teachers will have a strong foundation upon which to base word study instruction, evaluate students' needs and progress in reading, and make decisions about future instruction that will help students access content area texts. Word study instruction combines several areas of reading, that when taught together, can make students veritable word whizzes.

DISCUSSION QUESTIONS

1. Recall a time when you read something that was enjoyable. What were you reading? Why were you reading it? Relate these ideas to reader purpose, motivation, and attention. How can these ideas inform your selection of content texts and materials for your students?

2. When you are reading a text and realize you have poor comprehension, what do you do? What comprehension repair strategies work best for you? What about for your students? What strategies do they use?

CHAPTER 2

Reading Difficulties

Despite the implementation of federal policies focused on early intervention and prevention of reading difficulties (e.g., Head Start and Reading First), a large proportion of students, particularly those with disabilities, continues to enter middle and high schools with poor reading skills (Boardman et al., 2008; Deshler & Hock, 2007). As stated in the introduction, 63% of students with disabilities, 71% of English language learners, 42% of Black students, and 34% of Hispanic students read below basic level in 8th grade according to the National Assessment of Educational Progress (U.S. Department of Education, 2015).

Such statistics beg several questions. How is it possible that students continually enter middle and high school still reading well below grade level? How can we address the clear inequalities that emerge for students of diverse backgrounds? Can anything be done to help these students improve? The answers are fairly simple. At any point in the reading process (described in Chapter 1), students with or without disabilities can experience reading difficulties for a variety of reasons. For instance, some students with disabilities may struggle to decode text. Other students may decode text easily but have no comprehension of what they read. There are numerous potential underlying causes of these different problems, meaning a one-size-fits-all reading intervention is unlikely to address students' individualized needs (Bursuck & Damer, 2011). Without receiving intensive intervention targeting specific areas of need, students' reading problems will persist into adolescence and beyond (Lyon, 2000). In fact, Lyon (2003) states that "failure to develop basic reading skills by age nine predicts a lifetime of illiteracy (i.e., not being able to read well or at all). Unless these students receive the appropriate instruction, more than 74% of the children entering first grade who are at-risk for reading failure will continue to have reading problems into adulthood" (p. 17).

WHY DO SOME STUDENTS STRUGGLE WITH READING?

There are many reasons why students struggle with reading. Reading difficulties can be caused by intrinsic factors like disability; they can also be attributed to extrinsic or environmental factors (Vellutino, Fletcher, Snowling, & Scanlon, 2004).

Disability

Students identified with a specific learning disability in reading, by definition, have reading difficulties. But, not all students identified with disabilities have formal reading-related disabilities. Some students have attention-deficit/hyperactivity disorder (ADHD), emotional and behavioral disorders (EBD), or autism spectrum disorder (ASD), among others. These disability labels do not automatically mean students will struggle in reading, but they often do. For example, about 50% of students with ADHD experience reading problems (Yoshimasu et al., 2010). For these students, reading difficulties may occur because they cannot remain focused during classroom instruction or reading tasks. Students with EBD may exhibit challenging behaviors that result in being removed from the classroom, thereby missing out on instruction. As a result these students have large gaps in their reading skills and abilities. Research has also shown that children with hearing, speech, and language impairments are at risk for reading difficulties (Burns, Griffin, & Snow, 1999).

Diversity

As the nation's classrooms become more diverse, there is a growing mismatch between some students' background and traditional school expectations and pedagogies. Students who come from diverse linguistic, economic, cultural, or racial backgrounds may be disadvantaged because their home experiences, values, and expectations differ, and in some cases, are discounted by schools and teachers. When this occurs, students' academic success is jeopardized and reading is no exception.

English language learners (ELLs) from diverse linguistic backgrounds may struggle in reading if they have not attained a high enough level of English proficiency. After all, it is certainly difficult to successfully read a language that you do not speak. But even some ELLs who are more proficient in English continue to struggle in reading. Potential reasons for this include differences in the sounds and structures across languages, differences in cultural or background knowledge, and the use of figurative language like idioms (e.g., let the cat out of the bag). ELL students may struggle even more upon entering secondary classrooms because not only are they working to improve their English proficiency generally, but they are also trying to master the academic vocabulary that is essential in content area classes.

In addition to diverse linguistic backgrounds, students come from diverse economic backgrounds. In particular, students from low-socioeconomic status (SES) homes are at higher risk of reading difficulties for a variety of different reasons, including not having sufficient access to literacy-rich environments and experiences (more on this topic is in the section titled Early Language and Literacy Experiences), health care, housing, and food. In many of these students' homes, a parent or caregiver works multiple jobs to ensure the family's basic needs are met, leaving little time to help students practice reading at home.

Finally, students from diverse racial and cultural backgrounds disproportionately struggle in reading. This is in part due to cultural mismatches between families and schools. The ways families from diverse backgrounds value, define, and experience literacy may be different from formal, traditional school settings. In other cases, research has shown that educational personnel often have lower expectations for students from diverse cultural and racial backgrounds (Van den Bergh, Denessen, Hornstra, Voeten, & Holland, 2010) and are more likely to suspend and expel students from diverse cultural and racial backgrounds (Gregory, Skiba, & Noguera, 2010); both of these factors translate into lower reading achievement.

The "Matthew Effect"

In reading, the term *Matthew Effect*, coined by Stanovich (1986), is based on the parable of "the rich get richer and the poor get poorer" in the book of Matthew in the Bible (Chapter 25). Stanovich used the term Matthew Effect to describe accumulated advantage or disadvantage resulting from students' reading abilities. For poor readers, a vicious downward cycle occurs when students experience reading failure. Poor readers who do not like to read because it is difficult avoid reading. This avoidance ensures that they have few opportunities to practice and thereby improve. Because their reading does not improve, reading continues to be a negative experience for them, and the cycle repeats.

The opposite is true for students who are proficient readers (Stanovich, 1986). These students tend to enjoy reading and spend more time reading. Opportunities for extra practice mean good readers

EDITORIAL DEPT.

GLASBERGEN

"We'd like you to condense your novel into something that younger people will want to read...in 140 characters or less."

continually improve (see Figure 2.1). Recent research has shown the Matthew Effect is particularly pronounced with regard to students' vocabulary development (Cain & Oakhill, 2011). Students identified with poor comprehension skills at age 8 had reduced growth in vocabulary at ages 11, 14, and 16, compared to students with good comprehension skills at age 8. This study suggests that when it comes to students' vocabulary, rich readers get richer, and poor readers get poorer. This finding is particularly pertinent to this book's focus on reading in secondary content area classrooms as vocabulary is a critical component of disciplinary knowledge and language.

Early Language and Literacy Experiences

Let's revisit one of the questions I posed at the beginning of the chapter: *How is it possible students continue to enter middle and high school still reading well below grade level?* The sobering reality is that before some students enter school, they have already started down a path that disadvantages them in the area of reading. Considerable evidence indicates the quality and quantity of young children's early experiences with language and literacy are important influences on their reading success once they enter school (U.S. Department of Education, 2000). Young children who are read to frequently, have access to books and other print materials, and have stimulating literacy experiences enter school with better developed vocabularies, print awareness, and phonological awareness (Lyon, 2000). Young children who lack such exposure and experiences

Figure 2.1. The Matthew Effect for Good Readers

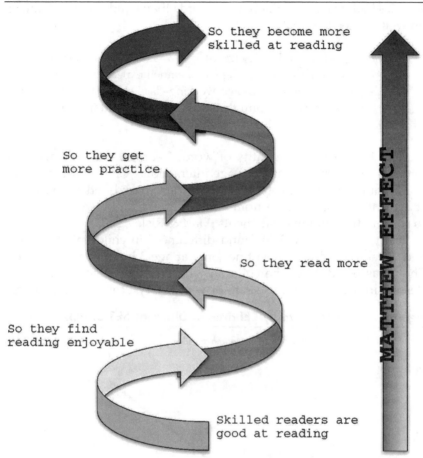

So they become more
skilled at reading

So they get
more practice

So they read more

So they find
reading enjoyable

Skilled readers are
good at reading

MATTHEW EFFECT

are not necessarily destined to experience reading difficulties, but they enter school already behind their peers and must begin "catching up" immediately (Lyon, 2000; U.S. Department of Education, 2000).

The same is true for early language experiences. Children who come from home environments in which they are spoken to often and involved in language experiences are better prepared to learn to read when they enter school (O'Connor, 2007). In a well-known longitudinal study, Hart and Risley (1995) followed 42 families representing three socioeconomic levels: professional, working, and welfare. Hart and Risley followed one child in each of these families from age 7 months to 3 years. The research team conducted monthly observations in the families' homes, recording the conversations and language experiences that involved the child study participants.

The results were striking. By age 3, children from high-income families had heard 30 million more words than children from families on welfare (see Figure 2.2).

> According to Hart and Risley (2003), in terms of "words heard, the average child on welfare was having half as much experience per hour (616 words per hour) as the average working-class child (1,251 words per hour) and less than one-third that of the average child in a professional family (2,153 words per hour)" (p. 8).

In addition to the quantity of words heard, there were also differences in the quality of language interactions. Children from higher SES families were likely to receive praise-based and encouraging statements, while children from families on welfare were more likely to receive discouraging statements (Hart & Risley, 2003).

Hart and Risley (2003) found differences in children's language and vocabulary development not only at age 3 but also at ages 9–10. They reassessed 29 of the children when they were in third grade. Results indicated children's rate of vocabulary growth at age 3 was

Figure 2.2. Words Heard by Children in Different SES Groups

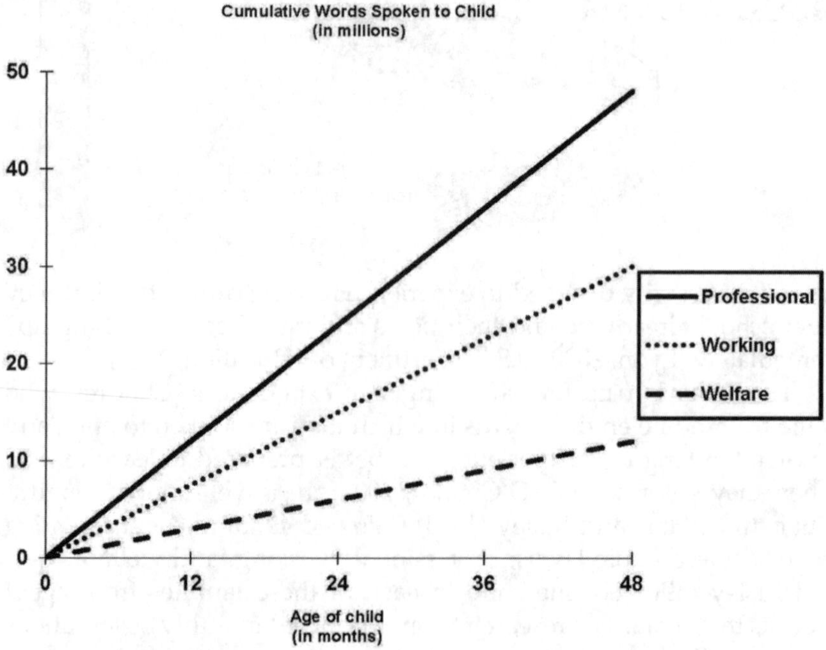

Note: Statistics from Hart & Risley (1995)

strongly associated with language skill, vocabulary development, and reading comprehension at age 9–10.

You may be wondering, what relevance does students' early language and literacy experience have for a book on word study in secondary classrooms? First, it is important to understand that some secondary students' reading struggles stem from issues of socioeconomic inequity present long before they entered kindergarten. These students have had to "catch up" to their more affluent peers from day one of entering school. Whenever I am in a middle or high school classroom and observe a student who is reluctant when asked to read or participate in reading-dependent activities, I automatically recall Hart and Risley's work. Given the critical role vocabulary plays in reading achievement, is it possible this student has a poor attitude because he or she entered school "behind" and has subsequently experienced years of reading failure? Second, research like that of Hart and Risley provides support for the importance of word study as a means of helping improve students' vocabulary development. Word study provides a way to help *all* students improve their word learning skills and vocabulary knowledge, even if their early language and literacy experiences disadvantage them compared to some of their peers. We must remember that adolescence is not too late to intervene (Scammacca et al., 2007), and providing word study instruction is a great way for all teachers to be involved.

Instruction and Assessment

Children are not born knowing how to read. It is a learned skill that is dependent on instructional quantity and quality (Kamhi & Catts, 2012). If children receive inadequate or poor quality reading instruction, they will likely struggle in reading. Think about a scenario in which you are trying to learn to read Korean. Read the following sentence:

안녕하십니까

Reading these characters is probably impossible to do unless you are already fluent in Korean. If, however, you are explicitly taught the Korean alphabet and word structure and then given plentiful opportunities to practice with corrective feedback—characteristics of high-quality reading instruction (Adams, 1990)—you will be more likely to learn to read Korean successfully and know that

안녕하십니까

means "how are you?"

If high-quality reading instruction is one side of the coin, then frequent assessment is the other. Teaching does not automatically result in learning. Determining whether teaching results in learning requires assessment. In other words, assessing students' learning is a way to assess whether instruction (i.e., teaching) is effective (Hamilton et al., 2009). When students' reading achievement and progress are not closely monitored, it is easy to overlook their instructional needs. For students who exhibit signs of reading difficulty, it is critical that teachers administer comprehensive and frequent assessments to determine students' specific areas of need (Connor, Alberto, Compton, & O'Connor, 2014; Rhodes & Shanklin, 1993).

Two types of assessment are critical: diagnostic and progress monitoring. Diagnostic assessments provide data on students' incoming knowledge and skill level (Bursuck & Damer, 2011). From diagnostic assessments teachers can determine what skills students have or have not mastered and then plan instruction accordingly. Progress monitoring is a way to determine if students are making learning progress based on the instruction they receive (Connor et al., 2014). Progress monitoring assessments also provide data that can be used to determine students' rate of growth (Deno, Fuchs, Marston, & Shin, 2001). If students are not improving at an acceptable rate, it is an indication that instruction is not properly addressing students' needs (Jenkins, Hudson, & Lee, 2007).

In terms of word study, it is important to understand what knowledge and skills students have acquired or are missing in the areas of decoding, spelling, and vocabulary so teachers can plan and implement instruction accordingly. For example, which prefixes do students know? Do students know the six syllable types? Assessment data will provide the answers, as I will show in Chapter 4.

PROBLEMS IN THE FIVE AREAS OF READING

Whatever the underlying cause of students' reading difficulties might be, one or more of the five areas of reading will be affected. Many times a deficit in one area will translate to deficits in other areas. For example, there is reliable evidence that word identification problems are related to deficiencies in phonological awareness and decoding that lead to difficulties in establishing relationships between a word's spoken and written parts (Vellutino et al., 2004). Determining students' particular areas of difficulty is critical to crafting instruction and intervention plans that will address students' needs in the most effective and efficient manner. For example, if assessment data indicate a student is not reading with fluency, providing a decoding intervention will not be of much help.

Efficient and automatic decoding enables individuals to read accurately and rapidly (NRP, 2000; O'Connor & Bell, 2004). The inability to decode text is often the result of poor phonemic awareness as well as a lack of phonics knowledge (Adams, 1990; Mercer & Pullen, 2005; O'Connor & Bell, 2004).

Fluency is closely tied to text comprehension (Strecker, Roser, & Martinez, 2005). Students who are fluent readers do not need to think consciously about decoding as they read, and therefore they are able to devote most of their attention to comprehending text. The opposite is true for students who do not read fluently. These students spend more time and attention decoding, thereby devoting less attention to comprehending.

Reading fluency problems can be attributed to several factors. First is a limited sight word vocabulary (Ehri & Snowling, 2004). Sight words are words that occur frequently and should be recognized automatically (i.e., by sight). If students have to stop to figure out a word, their attention is diverted from comprehending the text to decoding it. Second, fluency is disrupted if students have poor decoding skills and make a large number of mistakes during reading. Decoding mistakes are more likely among struggling readers or readers who are tackling a text that is too difficult for them (Ehri & Snowling, 2004).

Even if students are able to decode words easily and read them fluently, 20% of students with reading difficulties struggle to understand text because they do not understand the meanings of the words they read (Duke, Pressley, & Hilden, 2004). Limited background knowledge, or the lack of existing frames of reference, as well as limited vocabulary knowledge in general, reduce students' ability to gain meaning from text (Duke et al., 2004; Mercer & Pullen, 2005). To comprehend a text, students must understand a minimum of 90% of the words (Hirsch, 2005). Strongly related to vocabulary knowledge is background knowledge. As I pointed out in Chapter 1, background knowledge for a particular text increases students' familiarity with key vocabulary, enables students to create mental images of what they read, and helps students make personal connections to text. In fact, students' existing knowledge about subject matter "is probably the single most influential factor in what he or she will learn" (Alvermann, Phelps, & Ridgeway, 2007, p. 166).

Although many secondary students have entered middle and high school with underdeveloped reading skills, there are research-based strategies and interventions that can support their success, and all secondary teachers can play an active role. Word study instruction can address several barriers to comprehension (e.g., poor decoding and vocabulary knowledge) that struggling readers and students with disabilities face. Moreover, as I discuss in subsequent chapters, incorporating word study instruction in secondary classrooms will provide *all* students with tools to become independent word learners.

DISCUSSION QUESTIONS

1. Describe a time in your life when the Matthew Effect operated in either a positive or negative way.

2. In which areas of reading do the struggling readers and students with disabilities in your class struggle most? Do some of them read accurately but very slowly and without expression? Do some read quickly and accurately but have no comprehension of what they read? Or do some struggle to accurately decode the words in text? All of the above?

3. Why are early literacy and language experiences so important in young children's lives? How do these experiences relate to reading at the secondary level?

CHAPTER 3

American English
A System Governed by Rules Except for the Exceptions

Success with word study depends on knowing the basic parts of words that comprise American English and the rules that govern how those parts work together. The more students understand the origins of the American English language and the rules that govern how words are formed, the easier students will find decoding, spelling, and understanding multisyllabic words. Knowledge of the basic rules will also help students recognize exceptions to the rules and why those exceptions occur. Being up-front with students that exceptions can and do occur and then providing students with support as specific exceptions arise will not only improve students' reading abilities, but will also reduce students' frustration upon encountering words that do not follow traditional patterns or conventions. The information presented in this chapter provides background information and examples that teachers can draw from when specific word patterns or exception words occur in class.

American English is a language derived from Anglo-Saxon, Greek, and Latin roots (Henry, 2003). Words with Anglo-Saxon origins are typically short and related to daily life, and they often have silent letters that were once pronounced, such as *knee, gnat, wrist,* and *ghost*. The 100 most commonly used words in English have Anglo-Saxon origins (Moats, 2005). Words with Greek origins are often scientific words; based on Greek, /f/ is reliably spelled *ph* as in *photosynthesis* and /k/ is spelled *ch* as in *chemistry*. Words with Latin roots often appear in social studies and represent lofty ideas. For example *deo* (god) or *magni* (great) make up words like *deity* and *magnitude*.

Compared to other languages, American English is a fairly young language. Modern English is about 400 years old, dating back to 1600 (Henry, 2003); whereas Chinese is several thousands of years old (DeFrancis, 1984). The fact that modern English is young and derived from several other languages helps explain why it gets a reputation as being idiosyncratic, especially in terms of letter–sound correspondences. For example, read the following sentences:

> The dove dove in the pond.
> I object to that object being presented as evidence.
> Eight aunts ate apples while watching ants.

With sentences like these, it is easy to conclude that American English is a confusing, arbitrary language. Actually, American English is more predictable and rule-bound than many people think. In fact, 84% of English words follow the predictable letter–sound correspondence patterns (Moats, 2005). Yes, there are exceptions to the typical patterns or rules, but once students know the major patterns and conventions, they will find relatively few exceptions.

WHAT ARE WORDS MADE OF?

Words are simply collections of individual speech sounds, or *phonemes*, represented by particular printed letters, or *graphemes*. In English, there are approximately 44 phonemes, which are represented by the 26 letters (or combinations of letters) of the alphabet. Table 3.1 displays the 44 phonemes and corresponding graphemes.

Successful decoding is contingent on knowing the phonemes and graphemes. The good news is that this information can be directly taught to students, a topic explored more fully in Part II of this book. As discussed in Chapters 1 and 2, being a proficient decoder does not automatically result in successful comprehension. The areas of fluency and vocabulary also have important parts to play in the reading process. But *not* being a skilled and efficient decoder will almost certainly jeopardize comprehension.

Letter–Sound Correspondences

English letter–sound correspondences can be divided into consonant or vowel patterns, and single letters or combinations of letters represent these patterns. Teaching your students some of the ground rules governing these combinations can help them decode unfamiliar words.

Consonants. Sixteen letters represent a single consonant sound. For example, *d* is pronounced /d/, and *n* is pronounced /n/. Five letters (c, g, s, w, y) represent two sounds. In general, these single letter–sound correspondences are consistent.

"This company enthusiastically supports diversity, diversitee, divursity, divercity and dyversity."

There are some rules that can help students predict the correct sound for letters that have more than one sound.

1. Soft *c*: The letter *c* will make the /s/ sound when followed by the vowels *e*, *i*, or *y*. For example, *cedar, citation, receive, mice, cycle, spicy*. Otherwise the letter *c* makes the /k/ sound as in *cucumber, crystal, coast*.
2. Soft *g*: The letter *g* will make the /j/ sound when followed by the vowels *e*, *i*, or *y*. For example, *garage, gym, gel, ginger*. Otherwise the letter *g* makes the /g/ sound as in *grand, legacy, gallant*.
3. *S* making the /z/ sound: Usually occurs when the letter *s* follows a vowel. For example, *resident, surprise, busy*. Otherwise the letter *s* makes the /s/ sound as in *salamander, charters, soldier*.

What about words like *get, girl,* and *soccer*? These are exceptions and should be taught as such. Remember, English is a system governed by rules, except for the exceptions.

Consonant blends are groups of consonants in which each consonant retains its own individual sound. I tell students to think of these letter combinations as BFFs (best friends forever). Once together, they are not to be separated. *St-* is pronounced /s/ /t/, while *-nd* is pronounced /n/ /d/. Some consonant blends are made up of three adjacent consonants as in *spl-* which is pronounced /s/ /p/ /l/.

Consonant digraphs are two adjacent consonants that produce only one speech sound. *Sh* makes its own sound /sh/ as opposed to the

Table 3.1. Letter–Sound Correspondences

PHONEME	GRAPHEME(S)	EXAMPLE(S)
Consonant Letter–Sound Correspondences		
/b/	b	bat
/d/	d	dog
/f/	f, ph	fun, photo
/g/	g	good
/h/	h	hug
/j/	j, g, dge	jump, gel, edge
/k/	k, ck, c	kite, deck, cat
/l/	l, ll, le	lamp, full, cycle
/m/	m	mud
/n/	n, gn, kn	nap, gnat, knit
/p/	p	pet
/r/	r	rent
/s/	s, ss, c	sit, brass, cent
/t/	t	ten
/v/	v	vest
/w/	w, wh	well, when
/y/	y	yak
/z/	z, s	zoo, rise
Digraphs		
/ch/	ch	chair
/sh/	sh	shell
/th/ (unvoiced)	th	path
/th/ (voiced)	th	then
/kw/	qu	queen
/f/	ph	graph
/k/	-ck	clock
/n/	kn, gn	kneel, gnat
Trigraphs		
/ch/	-tch	fetch
/j/	-dge	-ledge

Table 3.1. Letter–Sound Correspondences (continued)

PHONEME	GRAPHEME(S)	EXAMPLE(S)
Vowel Letter–Sound Correspondences		
Short Vowels		
/a/	a	cat
/e/	e, ea	bet, bread
/i/	i	sit
/o/	o	dog
/u/	u	cut
Long Vowels		
/ā/	a-e, ai, ay	ate, mail, hay
/ē/	e-e, y, ea, ee	Pete, baby, meat, sleep
/ī/		
/ō/	i-e, y, igh	kite, try, night
/ū/	o-e, oa, ow	globe, boat, mow
	u-e,	mute
Dipthongs		
/ou/	ou, ow	house, cow
/oi/	oi, oy	coin, boy
Other Digraphs		
/au/	au, aw	cause, draw
/oo/	oo	boot
/oo/	oo	book
R- and L-Controlled		
/ar/	ar	park
/er/	er, ir, ur	her, bird, turn
/or/	or	corn
/au/ + /l/	al, all	royal, tall

individual sounds /s/ and /h/. *Ck* also makes one sound /k/. Some consonant digraphs make one sound because one letter is silent. *Kn–* is pronounced /n/ because the *k* is silent. There are also consonant trigraphs (three consonants representing one sound) as in *tch* which makes the /ch/ sound.

Vowels. When compared to consonants, vowels are not as predictable in terms of their letter–sound correspondences, and I always try to be up-front with students about the rather idiosyncratic nature of the vowels. Some general patterns, however, exist. The vowels *a, e, i, o, u,* and sometimes *y,* most often represent the short or long vowel sounds. If you wonder why the letter *y* is included with the vowels, think about the sound *y* makes in the following words: *try, baby, gym,* and *cycle.*

Vowels paired with the letter *r* are referred to as "*r*-controlled" vowels because the letter *r* changes the sound of the vowel. The letter *a* paired with *l* or *ll* is called "*l*-controlled" and produces a unique sound as in the word *tall.* Vowel digraphs are two adjacent vowels that produce one sound like the *oa* in *boat.* A special subgroup of vowel digraphs consists of dipthongs (*oy, oi, ou, ow*). These letter–sound correspondences have what is referred to as a "gliding phoneme" because the first sound glides into the second sound.

If you or your students need a brief tutorial on how to correctly pronounce the letter sounds, check out the video clips in the Tech Tip.

Tech Tip

Not sure how to correctly pronounce the letter sounds? Check out these video tutorials!

- www.youtube.com/
  watch?list=PLLxDwKxHx1yLfQFq0LsnzIK2JrrQRBfL9&v=Le9KrUfwmFk
- www.youtube.com/
  watch?list=PLLxDwKxHx1yLfQFq0LsnzIK2JrrQRBfL9&v=YGMmZx1fQZQ

Welded sounds. Welded sounds are groups of phonemes that operate as one unit, even though each grapheme represents an individual sound. I tell students to think of a sculpture in which various pieces of metal are welded or fused together. Thus, the phonemes in welded sounds are not separated easily. The welded sounds include these letter groups: *an, am, all, alk, ank, onk, unk, ing, ang, ong,* and *ung.*

Affixes

Affixes are small units of meaning that can be added to the beginning or end of words (called *base words*) to change their meaning. Affixes added to the beginning of a word are *prefixes.* Here are some examples:

Prefix	+	Base Word	=	New Word
Re	+	Try	=	Retry
Un	+	Done	=	Undone
Mid	+	Term	=	Midterm

Affixes added to the end of base words are called *suffixes*. Like prefixes, suffixes change the meaning of the base word.

Base Word	+	Suffix	=	New Word
Land	+	ed	=	Landed
Quick	+	ly	=	Quickly
Watch	+	ing	=	Watching

Affixes can also be added to parts of words referred to as *root words*. Root words carry meaning but cannot stand alone. They must be paired with a prefix, suffix, or both. For example, *ject* and *spect* are root words and are never used by themselves.

Prefix	+ Root Word	+ Suffix	= New Word
ob-	+ ject		= object
ob-	+ ject	+ -tion	= objection
in-	+ spect		= inspect
in-	+ spect	+ -or	= inspector

Regular vs. Irregular Words

Regular or decodable words are those with a direct one-to-one correspondence between the phonemes and graphemes and follow the "rules" of English. Sometimes regular words can seem tricky because they are special kinds of words: *Homographs* are words that are spelled the same but have different meanings (e.g., *desert* and *desert*); and *homophones* are words that are spelled differently but pronounced the same (e.g., *flower* and *flour*). Irregular words, on the other hand, do not follow the rules and cannot successfully be decoded by applying the typical phoneme–grapheme correspondences. They are also referred to as nonphonetic. It is best to be up-front with students about these words. Students should know that while many of the words they will encounter can be decoded according to standard phoneme–grapheme correspondences, others will simply have to be memorized.

Most often it is the vowel sound(s) that cause a word to be irregular. Sometimes irregular words are referred to as "sight words" because they must be memorized and recognized by sight as opposed to being decoded. In many cases, these words are irregular because they are derived from Anglo-Saxon, Greek, or Latin and have retained the original spelling patterns of these historic languages (Moats, 2005). Here is a list of examples of irregular words: *come, do, give, great, love, one, pear, pint, prove, said, spa, two.*

Proper nouns also have a tendency to be nonphonetic. For example, Kleenex is one of the only English words that begins with *kl.* Very few words begin with the letter x, but the company name Xerox does, and the *x* takes the /z/ sound. Some people's last names also fall in this category. Think about the names Boudreaux, Gonzales, Copland, and Dubois—all nonphonetic.

It is critical to never, never tell a student to "sound out" an irregular word. For example, if told to sound out the word *of,* a student will likely read *off.* Not only does this lead to the wrong word, but it also could result in students learning words incorrectly, both of which can contribute to students' lack of confidence as readers.

CONTINUAL EVOLUTION OF LANGUAGE

It is important for students to remember that American English is a language resulting from the combination of many other languages, and it is a language that is continually evolving. Some of the exceptions to certain rules come from the adoption of words from other languages and cultures (Henry, 2003). The words *chic, cuisine, encore,* and *souvenir* came to us from French, while *bravo, finale,* and *stiletto* are Italian; hence they do not follow traditional phonetic patterns.

As the population of the United States becomes increasingly diverse, American English will continue to evolve to accommodate new cultures and cultural traditions. I always remind students of the widespread immigration that occurred in the 19th and 20th centuries. As immigrants entered the country, they brought new ideas, sports, music, food—and words. Words like *taco, chow mein, gumbo, crepe, sushi, bratwurst,* and *bagel* are just a few of the many food words that originated from other countries but are now as "American" as apple pie.

English has also evolved based on discovery, innovation, and technological advances. The words *leotard, pasteurize, galvanize,* and *maverick* are all based on historical figures' names and a particular event for which they are known. The word *selfie* was nonexistent prior to about 2010, but it is now a common term in a world of communication through mobile devices and smartphones. We can thank social media and Twitter for *hashtag*. New technology gave us *microchip*, *laptop*, and *iPod*. Previously existing words have also taken on new meanings based on technological advances. *Plasma* is now pertinent to television screens. Phones are charged on *docks*, and *tablets* can play movies and music. The evolution of English based on innovation and technological advances will most likely continue unabated in the future as we must name the innovations that we discover and create.

Finally, American English has also evolved based on the use of *slang*, informal language often used in particular contexts or by particular groups of people. Neighborhoods are referred to as *hoods*, guy friends are *bros*, and foods are *delish*. People from the South are *fixin' to* go to the store, while folks from California are glad the store is not *hella* far away, and New Englanders think the store is *wicked* good. Gotta love English!

I have found that older students like the idea that they can and do contribute to the evolution of American English through slang. As a middle school teacher I remember having to be schooled by my students on what the latest slang meant, but now there are online resources to help. Ever feel like your students are speaking a different "slanguage"? Need a quick translation tool? Try the online slang dictionary shown in the Tech Tip.

TECH TIP

Need to keep up with the latest slang so you can understand your students? Check out the online slang dictionary: onlineslangdictionary.com

---

It is important for students to keep in mind that slang originates in informal communication, and is therefore not likely to follow traditional decoding and spelling patterns. In essence, slang and other words that originate from the continual evolution of American English add to a growing list of nonphonetic words that must be recognized by sight. Slang holds particular importance for ELL students. When words are used as slang, they often do not maintain their traditional meanings, which can cause difficulty for students who are learning English. For example, some ELL students might not understand how something can be *wicked* and *good* at the same time.

Although American English has a reputation for being irregular and difficult to learn, it is actually very predictable. This is good news for teachers of word study. Teaching the predictable decoding and spelling patterns will apply to hundreds of words. Thus, with a little instructional investment, students will have knowledge that can be generalized to other similar words. For example, if the word *decoy* appears in the text, teaching students the sound of /oy/ will help them decode not only *decoy* but other words like *deploy, employment, voyage,* and *loyal.* With this type of instruction struggling readers and students with disabilities can become more independent readers and learners within general education content area classrooms.

DISCUSSION QUESTIONS

1. How would you describe the role social media (e.g., Facebook, Twitter) plays in the continual evolution of American English?

2. How would you respond to the statement: "Teaching students phonics is pointless because English doesn't follow predictable rules."?

3. What is meant by "letter–sound correspondences"? Why is it critical for students to learn them?

4. What are some new words your students use that contribute to the evolution of American English? Where did these words come from?

5. Have your students ever used a slang term that was unfamiliar to you? If so, relate this experience to English language learners learning English.

Part II

THE NUTS AND BOLTS OF WORD STUDY

CHAPTER 4

Getting Started

For word study instruction to be most effective and seamlessly embedded in content area classrooms, there are several instructional principles and practices that I recommend implementing. The principles and practices presented in this chapter have been vetted through research with struggling readers and students with disabilities, but I have found that these principles of effective instruction can benefit all students in general education classes.

INSTRUCTIONAL PRINCIPLES

Extensive research supports a series of instructional principles and practices known to support the learning of struggling learners and students with disabilities. In this section we will learn about those that are particularly relevant for word study instruction.

Explicit Instruction

It is important that word study instruction is explicit, meaning that students are directly taught the individual word parts and skills. Asking students to guess how to decode the suffix -*tion* is *not* explicit. Telling them -*tion* is read as /shun/ is explicit. When students are asked to guess how to pronounce certain word parts or what they mean, valuable instructional time can be lost if students guess incorrectly. Even more detrimental is the fact that when students make errors, they risk learning the material incorrectly. In these cases teachers have to reteach the skill and often must overcome the frustration students experience because they made mistakes. Research has shown that reteaching errors becomes more difficult as students get older. Some estimates are that for high school students, reteaching errors takes three times the effort compared to simply setting up situations so students learn correctly in the first place (Bursuck & Damer, 2011; Engelmann, 1999). Teaching explicitly saves time and leads to more positive learning experiences for students and teachers. Here is an example of explicit instruction when teaching the prefix *inter-*.

> *(Teacher writes* inter- *on board.)*
>
> **Teacher:** This is the prefix *inter*. Listen again.
>
> *(Teacher points to inter-.)*
>
> **Teacher:** This prefix is *inter*. Let's try it together.
>
> *(Teacher points to inter- again.)*
>
> **Teacher:** What is this prefix?
> **Student:** Inter.
> **Teacher:** Yes! It is *inter*.
>
> *(Teacher writes* inter- = between *on the board. Teacher points to the writing on the board.)*
>
> **Teacher:** The prefix *inter* means between. Listen again. The prefix *inter* means between. Let's try it together.
>
> *(Teacher points to* between *on board.)*
>
> **Teacher:** What does the prefix *inter* mean?
> **Student:** Between.
> **Teacher:** Excellent. The prefix *inter* means between. Let's give everyone an individual turn.
>
> *(Teacher points to* inter- *on board.)*
>
> **Teacher:** Marcus. Your turn. What is this prefix?
> **Student:** Inter.
> **Teacher:** Great job! Yes, it is *inter*.
>
> *(Teacher points to* between *on board.)*
>
> **Teacher:** Taylor. Your turn. What does *inter* mean?
> **Student:** Between.
> **Teacher:** Yes! Wonderful. *Inter* means between.

A common way to refer to the above instructional sequence from a teacher's perspective is My Turn–Together–Your Turn (Bursuck & Damer, 2011). If you notice, first the teacher explicitly teaches students how to decode *inter-* (My Turn). The My Turn step can also be completed when teachers show or model for students how to use a strategy (several word study strategies are discussed in Chapter 5). Next, the teacher asks all students to participate as a group (Together). Finally, the teacher provides opportunities for students to respond individually (Your Turn). Using My Turn–Together–Your Turn will help reduce the likelihood students will make mistakes or learn something incorrectly. This instructional routine is powerful but does require time to ensure students have successfully learned information. In terms of word study there will not be enough time in a school day or year to teach every possible word part or new vocabulary term using this approach. Teachers need to make critical decisions about which specific skills, vocabulary, and strategies will be most beneficial to students in their class and then organize their instructional time around those key competencies (see Chapter 7 for more on this subject).

Systematic Instruction

Closely tied to explicit instruction is systematic instruction. Word study instruction should be systematic, meaning that the sequence of skills progresses from simple to more complex. It is best not to present students with instruction in more complex skills if they have not mastered preceding foundational skills. This includes not asking students to decode or determine the meanings of words that are comprised of unfamiliar word parts. For example, if students do not know that the prefix *inter-* means between, I would not recommend asking them to tell you the meanings of the words *intercept, intergalactic,* or *interpersonal.* Teachers will know what word study concepts and skills students already know by administering formal and teacher-created assessments, as I will discuss later in this chapter.

Immediate Feedback

Even with the best explicit, systematic instruction, students may make mistakes. When this occurs, it is important to provide immediate error correction. Otherwise, students are likely to continue making the same mistake. When providing error correction, I recommend (a) pointing out the error, (b) reteaching or reminding students of the skill or concept, (c) providing an immediate opportunity for students to practice, and (d) providing follow-up opportunities for practice over the subsequent few days or even weeks until I am sure students have learned and can correctly apply the skill or concept. I try to use students' errors as opportunities for teachable moments. For example, if I notice a student has spelled the word *paralegal* as "*perilegal,*" rather than simply telling the student how to correctly spell the word, I create an instructional opportunity by teaching or reviewing the relevant word study concepts. In this instance I would take the time to teach the student the prefix *para-*.

Positive Learning Environments

Middle and high school students who are struggling readers or have disabilities have probably experienced years of challenges in the area of reading. Unless teachers establish a positive learning environment, these students will not be motivated to engage in reading-dependent tasks. A positive learning environment is one in which all students feel they are welcome, successful, and smart. Moreover, these environments are structured around clear expectations and instructional practices that increase student motivation and engagement.

Establishing a positive learning environment can take many forms. Simply providing explicit, systematic instruction in word study may increase some students' success in reading, and this feeling of success may be all the motivation they need. Positive learning environments can also be established by delivering more praise and positive reinforcement instead of reprimands and criticisms. Students benefit more when they are told what they are doing well. Praising even small accomplishments can be instrumental in initiating an upward cycle of positivity in the classroom. The following are some examples of praised-based statements:

1. I appreciate how you took out your textbook the first time I asked.
2. I love how well Stacia, Renee, and Beth are working together on their research project.
3. Fabulous job answering question number 4 using your graphic organizer.
4. I knew you could do it! You read that word all by yourself.

Still another way to establish a positive learning environment is to implement a motivational system in which students identify a goal and, upon attaining the goal, receive a reward. Keep in mind this kind of a motivational system is only effective if students are motivated by the reward. Promising a student who is bored by computers 5 minutes of free time on the computer for completing an assignment will not be reinforcing. If you do not already know what is motivating for your students, ask them. I have found most students are more than happy to share what they like.

Motivational systems can be used with the entire class or just selected students who need extra support. In either case keep in mind that goals must be realistic. Offering a reward to a struggling reader for never making a decoding mistake for an entire year would be difficult, if not impossible, to attain. Setting a student up for failure in this way will do more harm than good in the long run because it could reinforce students' negative feelings about their reading abilities.

When first implementing a motivational system it is best to start with a series of small goals that students can attain fairly quickly. Experiencing near immediate success can help students "buy in" to the idea that their positive actions and efforts result in a good outcome. For some extremely reluctant readers, setting a goal of reading one sentence or paragraph may be necessary to start the momentum. For other students, completing all assigned work during one class period may be appropriate. Gradually, you can establish more ambitious learning and behavioral goals that students can work toward over longer periods of time. Perhaps instead of completing all assigned work during one class period, students could be rewarded when they have completed all assigned work for seven class periods.

SMALL-GROUP INSTRUCTION

Research has shown students with disabilities experience more academic and behavioral success when they receive instruction in small groups (Elbaum, Vaughn, Hughes, Moody, & Schumm, 2000; Foorman & Torgesen, 2001; Lane, Wehby, et al., 2003). In fact, a comprehensive review of secondary mathematics practices found more positive effects on student achievement when teachers used cooperative learning groups (Slavin, Lake, & Groff, 2009). Yet, in many secondary classrooms I visit, whole-group, teacher-directed, lecture-based, and passive learning is often the status quo, and research has shown this is quite common across the country (Goodlad, 2004).

By implementing small-group instruction on a more regular basis, teachers will have more opportunities to provide students with (and without) disabilities differentiated instruction in the word study strategies presented in this book. Some of the benefits of differentiated small-group instruction include opportunities for:

1. teachers to listen to students practice reading aloud in a less intimidating environment,
2. teachers to provide immediate feedback and error correction,
3. teachers to provide minilessons on skills or content to particular groups of students who need them,
4. teachers to conduct running record assessments,

5. students to learn from one another, and
6. students to take leadership roles in their learning interactions with one another.

Small-group instruction also results in higher student engagement and achievement for students with and without disabilities (Al Otaiba et al., 2011; Lou et al., 1996; Vaughn, Hughes, Moody, and Elbaum, 2001). Table 4.1 provides resources on several research-based strategies for implementing small-group, cooperative learning in classrooms.

Peer Assisted Learning (PALS; see kc.vanderbilt.edu/pals/) is a strategy to support students' reading. In the PALS strategy peers work together in pairs or small groups to sequence information, generate main idea statements, and generate and evaluate text predictions. Students also learn how to correct their group members' reading errors (Fuchs, Fuchs, Mathes, & Simmons, 1997; Rafdal, McMaster, McConnell, Fuchs, & Fuchs, 2011). ClassWide Peer Tutoring (CWPT; see www.specialconnections.ku.edu/?q=instruction/classwide_peer_tutoring) is a strategy to promote content area learning. Students learn how to work in pairs as tutors and tutees to reinforce content learning (e.g., vocabulary terms, multiplication facts). ClassWide Peer Tutoring also incorporates a whole-class motivational system (Delquadri, Greenwood, Stretton, & Hall, 1983; Maheady, & Gard, 2010). Reciprocal Teaching (see www.readingrockets.org/strategies/reciprocal_teaching) is similar to PALS in that students learn how to work together to comprehend text. In this strategy students are assigned a role as summarizer, questioner, clarifier, or predictor, and they carry out these roles to read and comprehend a series of passages from a text (Palincsar, 2012; Palincsar & Brown, 1984). Finally, Collaborative Strategic Reading (CSR; see www.readingrockets.org/strategies/reciprocal_teaching) is designed to improve students' comprehension of content area texts. Students

Table 4.1. Resources for Small-Group Strategies

Strategy	Resource
Peer Assisted Learning (PALS)	kc.vanderbilt.edu/pals/
ClassWide Peer Tutoring (CWPT)	www.specialconnections.ku.edu/?q=instruction/classwide_peer_tutoring
Reciprocal Teaching	www.readingrockets.org/strategies/reciprocal_teaching
Collaborative Strategic Reading (CSR)	www.readingrockets.org/article/using-collaborative-strategic-reading

work in small groups and implement a series of reading strategies including text previewing, comprehension monitoring, summarizing, and generating main ideas (Klingner & Vaughn, 1996; Vaughn, Klingner, et al., 2011).

ASSESSMENT

Knowing your students' strengths and weaknesses in word study will be instrumental in designing effective, responsive instruction. Also important is evaluating the level of difficulty of the texts and curricular materials you use in your class. Data that result from the assessments described in the next sections provide information that can explain why students may be struggling to read and understand content area texts.

Assessing Students

For word study instruction to be effective and a good use of instructional time, it must address the skills and knowledge students need. Struggling readers and students with disabilities may be proficient in some skills but need more instruction in others. These students also tend to need instruction in foundational skills necessary for efficient, accurate decoding of multisyllabic words. Collecting assessment data will help you determine where to begin with your word study instruction. Luckily, there are several assessments that are readily available and easy to administer that can provide data to help focus instruction.

- *CORE Phonics Survey.* This assessment of phonics and spelling takes about 10 minutes to administer. Students read words from a series of lists based on letter–sound correspondences or word parts including individual letter sounds, blends, digraphs, and syllable types. There is a specific section on multisyllabic words, as well as a section on spelling. Data from this assessment can help you identify the specific word study skills students have acquired or are missing. Assessment available at www.scholastic.com/dodea/Module_2/resources/dodea_m2_tr_core.pdf
- *San Diego Quick Assessment of Reading Ability.* This 10-minute assessment provides an estimation of students' grade-level reading ability. Students read leveled word lists that will identify approximately which grade-level texts

they can read independently or with assistance. Assessment available at facstaff.bloomu.edu/dwalker/Documents/San%20Diego%20Quick%20Assessment.pdf

- **CORE Vocabulary Screening.** This vocabulary assessment takes 10–20 minutes to complete. It will provide data on how well students can read and understand the meanings of grade-level vocabulary. This assessment is not a measure of students' knowledge of content area vocabulary but rather a general indication of whether their vocabulary knowledge is on par with other students. Assessment available at www.corelearn.com/Products/Publications
- **Upper-Level Spelling Inventory.** This spelling assessment takes about 10–20 minutes to administer. Students spell words that are leveled and include the major spelling patterns, word parts, and affixes. The data resulting from this assessment will let you know which word study skills students have mastered or need to learn. Assessment available at readingandwritingproject.com/public/resources/assessments/spelling/spelling_upper.pdf

Additional more formal assessments are:
- Test of Word Reading Efficiency (TOWRE) available at www.pearsonclinical.co.uk/Psychology/generic/TestofWordReadingEfficiency(TOWRE)/TestofWordReadingEfficiency(TOWRE).aspx
- AIMS Web available at www.aimsweb.com
- DIBELS Nonsense Word Fluency (NWF) available at dibels.uoregon.edu/assessment/dibels/measures/nwf.php
- EasyCBM available at www.easycbm.com

You can also create your own assessments that are specific to your particular content area. You can create vocabulary or spelling pretests that assess students' incoming knowledge of the important vocabulary terms you plan to teach in an upcoming lesson or unit.

Assessing Texts

Just because a textbook is designed for a particular grade level does not mean that the actual text is written on the appropriate level. In my experience, many textbooks used in middle school classrooms are actually written on high school levels or higher. In such cases, it is little wonder that struggling readers and students with disabilities struggle to keep up in general education content area classrooms. As such, it is a good idea to evaluate the level of difficulty of the texts and curricular materials used in your classroom. By doing so, you will know when you will need to provide more support for texts that are above grade level or disproportionately difficult.

One way to evaluate a text is to calculate its readability, which is a measure of text difficulty. Most readability estimates are determined based on a proportion of average sentence length to average word length as measured by number of either letters or syllables. Longer sentences that contain many long words are more difficult to read and therefore are considered to be on a higher reading grade level. See Table 4.2 for online sources for some methods of calculating readability

Although you can calculate a text's readability by hand, it would be tedious and time consuming to do on a regular basis. Luckily there are several free online calculators that allow you to simply cut and paste a sample passage from a text. Then the online calculator will do the rest of the work.

TECH TIP

Go to these websites to access online readability calculators:

- Readability-Score.com: readability-score.com
- The Readability Test Tool: read-able.com
- Readability Calculator: www.online-utility.org/english/readability_test_and_improve.jsp

---

I present information on readability estimates and calculators to provide teachers with tools to better analyze texts in relation to students' abilities; however, several cautions are warranted. Readability estimates are simply that—estimates. There is a whole body of research that has focused on the accuracy, or lack thereof, of readability estimates (e.g., see Hiebert & Mesmer, 2013). So while readability estimates may provide some useful information on text characteristics, keep in mind that these estimates do not take into account individual learners and context. A chemistry text written about atoms and ions might score at an easier readability level because the words *atoms* and *ions* are relatively short. However, if students do not have any background information about the topic and do not know what atoms and ions are, this text will actually be much harder to read and understand than it might appear.

Table 4.2. Sources for Methods of Calculating Readability

Readability Estimate	Website	Notes
Dale-Chall	www.readabilityformulas.com/free-dale-chall-test.php	Assesses materials above 4th grade level
Ragor Estimate	www.readabilityformulas.com/the-raygor-estimate-graph.php	Assesses materials at or above 3rd grade level
Fry Method	www.readabilityformulas.com/fry-graph-readability-formula.php	Assesses materials at or above 1st grade level
Flesch-Kincaid (using Microsoft Word)	https://support.office.com/en-us/article/Test-your-document-s-readability-0ad-c0e9a-b3fb-4bde-85f4-c9e-88926c6aa	Directions for how to obtain readability estimate directly from Microsoft Outlook and Office

This leads us to a second way of assessing texts—assessing texts in relation to individual student abilities. The chemistry text about atoms and ions referenced above could be very challenging for some students while at the same time being easily read and understood by other students. To determine the appropriateness of a text for an individual student, experts often use a system that classifies texts according to difficulty. Texts are categorized according to whether they are on students' independent, instructional, or frustration level (Tyner, 2009). Books at students' independent level are ones that students can read with 98–100% accuracy. For example, given a 100-word passage, a text would be considered "independent level" if a student could read the passage with two or fewer errors. Students can read texts at this level without assistance. Instructional level texts are those students can read with 93–97% accuracy. These texts are appropriate for students only if they have a teacher or more advanced reader supporting them. Finally, texts at students' frustration level are ones that students struggle to read and result in accuracy rates below 93%. Students should never be asked to read a text that is on their frustration level.

You can quickly calculate the level of difficulty of a text for an individual student by administering a "running record." Running records provide information on how well students can read specific texts by recording the errors students make. Running records are convenient to administer because they can be completed in about 10 minutes or less and can be conducted using any text. Here are the steps for conducting a running record:

Step 1: Count the first one hundred words in a text.
Step 2: Ask the student to read aloud the 100 words, and as the student reads aloud, tally the number of errors made.
Step 3: Once the student has finished reading, subtract the total number of errors from 100 and then divide by 100.
Step 4: Use the percentage calculated in Step 3 to determine whether the text is at the student's independent (98–100%= 2 or less errors), instructional (93–97%= 3–7 errors), or frustration level (below 93%= 8 or more errors).

You can take the basic running record one step further and collect qualitative data on the types of errors students make. Instead of just tallying the number of errors, you can record the specific decoding errors students make for later analysis. When I conduct a running record, I record a check mark for each word students decode correctly. If students make errors, I record exactly what they say so I can get a sense of what difficulties they are experiencing. Here's an example:

✓ ✓ ✓ ✓ legal-ation ✓ ✓

In this case the student correctly read six words and incorrectly read the word *legislation* as "legal-ation." Figure 4.1 presents a completed sample running record.

What happens if you discover many of the texts used in your classroom are at some students' frustration level? The answer involves a combination of making the texts more accessible while also providing students with alternative texts that are easier to read. To make texts more accessible, you can select texts or curricular materials that have companion electronic versions so students can have the texts read aloud to them on a computer or iPad. Luckily supplemental digital and online resources come fairly standard with most textbook packages. You can also scan a text so students can use the text-to-speech feature on computers. Finding the Speech feature on computers is relatively easy. For PCs this feature is accessed from the Control Panel on the Start menu. For Macs it is located on the System Preferences menu.

You can also provide students with alternative texts that are written on easier reading levels. In recent years some publishing companies have made implementing this option much easier. These companies

TECH TIP	
Most PC and Mac computers come equipped with speech-to-text and text-to-speech programs.	
For PCs	**For Macs**
Option 1 • Go to Start • Click on Control Panel • Select Preferred View • Locate sound connections and connect jack to computer • Go to Start again • Click on Control Panel • Double-click Speech • Click on Text-to-Speech • Click on Audio Output **Option 2** • Type *Speech* in the Search tool found on the Start page • Select Windows Speech Recognition	• Open System Preferences • Click on Speech • Click on Text-to-Speech

are producing a greater number of books that meet older students' reading needs *and* appeal to their interests. Experts label such books as "high-interest low-readability" (Biancarosa & Snow, 2006). Some of these texts have reading levels as low as 1st grade-enabling older students who are reading several years below grade level to participate successfully in reading instruction. Often high-interest low-readability books resemble the chapter books or novels that on-grade-level peers might read; thus struggling readers and students with disabilities are more willing to participate in reading instruction, because they are not embarrassed by having to read books that look like they are intended for younger students. High-interest low-readability books span a variety of genres including fiction, nonfiction, poetry, and graphic novels. Table 4.3 provides a list of publishers who market high-interest low-readability texts. In terms of English/language arts, several of these companies have modified classic works of literature by authors like Shakespeare, Hemingway, and Dickens. For science and social

Figure 4.1. Sample Running Record

Student: **Matthew** Date: **9-29-15**

Text: *Scholastic News: Courageous Climber*

✓	✓	✓	✓	✓	✓	✓	✓	✓	✓
✓	✓	✓	✓	✓	✓	✓	✓	✓	✓
✓	✓	✓	✓	✓	✓	✓	✓	✓	✓
wooded	waror	✓	✓	✓	✓	✓	✓	✓	✓
✓	✓	✓	✓	✓	✓	✓	✓	✓	✓
✓	✓	✓	✓	grape	✓	✓	✓	✓	✓
✓	✓	✓	✓	✓	✓	✓	✓	✓	✓
✓	✓	✓	✓	✓	✓	✓	✓	✓	✓
✓	✓	✓	✓	✓	✓	form	✓	✓	✓
✓	✓	✓	✓	✓	✓	✓	✓	✓	✓

ACCURACY: 100 - 4 = **96** / 100 = **96** %

Independent	**Instructional**	**Frustration**
(98–100%)	(93–97%)	(92% and lower)

Error Analysis

Error	Target Word	Error	Target Word
wooded	wounded	waror	warrior
grape	grappling	form	formation

Note: A blank reproducible version of this figure is available for free download at www.tcpress.com

studies, these companies have a wide selection of expository texts about content commonly taught in these subject areas.

It is important to issue a word of caution regarding making texts more accessible to the struggling readers and students with disabilities in your classes. Providing students with a lower-grade-level text or allowing students to listen to a text read aloud to them would be considered accommodations in many school districts. Whether or not

Table 4.3. Publishing Companies That Sell High-Interest Low-Readability Texts

Company	Website that Links to High-Interest Low-Readability Books	Range of Products (in grade levels)
High Noon	www.highnoonbooks.com/inside-readers.tpl?cart=13212940611972 9	Interest levels: 3–12 Reading levels: 1–6
EDCON Publishing Group	www.edconpublishing.com/index.php?route=product/category&path=14	Interest levels: 3–12 Reading levels: 1–6
HIP Books	www.hip-books.com	Interest levels: 3–12 Reading levels: 2–4
National Reading Styles Institute (nrsi.com)	store.nrsi.com/catalogsearch/result/?q=high+interest+books+-for+struggling+readers&x=0&y=0	Interest levels: pre-K–10 Reading levels: pre-K–7
Perfection Learning	www.perfectionlearning.com/browse.php?categoryID=3929&level=2&parent=2543	Interest level: 2–12 Reading levels: 1–6
Saddleback Educational	http://www.sdlback.com/hi-lo-reading/hi-lo-reading-fiction/grade-level/elementary	Interest level: 4–9 Reading levels: 1–6
Scholastic	http://www.scholastic.com/parents/blogs/scholastic-parents-raise-reader/high-interest-books-struggling-middle-school-readers	Interest levels: 4–12 Reading levels: 1–12
Steck Vaughn/Houghton Mifflin Harcourt	steckvaughn.hmhco.com/en/adolesliteracy.htm	Interest levels: 4–12 Reading levels: 2–11
Sundance	www.sundancepub.com/c/@fr6bQVs_ZMevk/Pages/product.html?record@S3443	Interest levels: 2–8 Reading level: 1–8

students qualify for specific accommodations is sometimes a decision that requires the approval of members of Individualized Education Program (IEP) teams for students with disabilities or other school-level problem-solving teams. Check with the appropriate person or team at your school before implementing specific accommodations for students.

Word study instruction will be most powerful if it is implemented in classrooms that are positive learning environments for all students, but in particular for struggling readers and students with disabilities. By incorporating the principles and strategies of effective, appropriate, and engaging instruction you will have already completed the lion's share of work in setting your students up for success.

DISCUSSION QUESTIONS

1. What do you do to reward yourself when you attain a goal? Would you continue working if you no longer received a paycheck? Relate these ideas to establishing a motivational system in your classroom.

2. What are some ways you establish a positive learning environment in your classroom? Are there particular rewards that students find motivating?

3. To what extent do you incorporate small-group, cooperative learning in your classroom? Discuss the benefits of this format.

4. What genres do the students in your classes enjoy reading most? What topics are their favorites? Do they have access to texts that they find interesting and can read successfully?

5. To what extent do you incorporate digital and online resources in your instruction? Are there some resources you would like to try?

6. Take a moment to try out some of the online readability estimates. Select a passage from a text you use often in your classroom. Did the results surprise you?

CHAPTER 5

Word Study Methods and Strategies

The ability to decode multisyllabic words is essential for students as they read, write, and learn in all areas of school and life. Many multisyllabic words occur infrequently, but when they do occur, they convey the bulk of the meaning of what is being read (Cunningham, 1998). So if students cannot decode and determine the meaning of these words, their comprehension is doomed. Take for example, the following sentence:

In a right _____, the _____ is _____ the right _____.

The blanks represent multisyllabic words, and although there are only three of them, they carry the bulk of the meaning for the sentence. Not having the requisite advanced word study skills to decode these words means that adolescents with disabilities will be unable to comprehend this sentence. Likewise, they will also have little comprehension of longer content area texts. This simulates what secondary students with disabilities might experience when trying to read a geometry textbook. Deciphering the meaning of this sentence would take a lot of time and effort and probably many random guesses. Once you are able to decode the multisyllabic words, however, the meaning becomes apparent. Try the sentence now.

In a right triangle the hypotenuse is opposite the right angle.

Advanced word study—decoding, spelling, and vocabulary knowledge of multisyllabic words—is a critical component of instruction. Helping adolescents with disabilities become proficient in the area of advanced word study is crucial to their success at the secondary level (Boardman et al., 2008; Scammacca et al., 2007).

Students with disabilities who struggle in reading may not have acquired this skill. So when they encounter a word like *thermometer* they might randomly guess a word that starts with the letter *t*, or they might just skip the word entirely. In either case, they will not be able to comprehend the text because they cannot decode the word, much less determine its meaning. This is particularly problematic because, as students advance in grade levels, they encounter more challenging, multisyllabic words. In fact, starting around 4th grade, curricular materials are written at increasingly advanced levels with the idea that students are "reading to learn" as opposed to "learning to read" (Chall, Jacobs, & Baldwin, 1990).

I have worked with many adolescents with disabilities who can decode and understand basic single-syllable words or high-frequency words. When they encounter longer, more complicated, or rare words, however, they struggle to accurately decode them and break them apart to determine meaning. For adolescents with disabilities, reading and understanding multisyllabic words is a critical skill for succeeding in general education content area classrooms.

METHODS FOR DECODING UNKNOWN WORDS

Take a look at the word *magnetohydrodynamic*. Unless you are a scientist who generates electricity by passing an ionized gas though a magnetic field at an extremely high temperature, this word is probably unfamiliar to you. Yet, you can probably decode it. Perhaps you looked for smaller words or word parts you recognize like *magnet, hydro*, and *dynamic* and then put them together. Or maybe you grouped word parts together as you read the word from left to right. It is also possible that you are not exactly sure how you decoded the word. You just did. You might even have been able to make some educated guesses about what parts of the word mean.

It is estimated that during their school careers, students will encounter over 88,000 words (Nagy & Anderson, 1984), with the majority being two syllables or more (Cunningham, 1998). This is too many words for students to memorize by rote or learn as sight words. To tackle decoding so many unfamiliar words requires a set of strategies that students can flexibly apply in a variety of contexts. Explicitly relating this idea to students can be powerful. If students understand that there are simply too many words to learn one at a time, they are often more motivated to learn and apply word study strategies. This is even true for nonstruggling readers.

Identifying Known Parts

One basic strategy is for students to look for known or familiar word parts in multisyllabic words. While this can be a simple strategy to implement, it is dependent on students' existing word knowledge and vocabulary.

The easiest words to use with this strategy are compound words, or words made up of two or more smaller words. *Doghouse, mailman,* and *gatekeeper* are examples of compound words. When presented with a compound word, students should be directed to divide between the two words and then read the smaller words from left to right. Here are a few examples:

Spacecraft	=	space / craft
Earthquake	=	earth / quake
Railroad	=	rail / road

Below is an example of how a teacher might assist a student decoding the compound word *foothill.*

(Teacher points to foothill *in book.)*

Teacher: Do you see any small words you recognize?
Student: Foot.
Teacher: Good. Do you see any other words?
Student: Hill.
Teacher: Right. Now put them together.
Student: Foot. Hill.
Teacher: Okay, now say it fast.
Student: Foothill.
Teacher: Yes! Foothill.

Other times students can identify one or more word parts and then put the parts together. For example, students might recognize *fact* or *factor* in the word *factorial,* or perhaps they can pick out *pass* in the word *passage.* They might also see parts of a word that remind them of other words. For example, if students know the words *microbe* and *telescope,* then through analogy, they can decode *microscope.* One caution, however, is that using known parts to decode new multisyllabic words does not work accurately with all words. Take the word *longitudinal.* Students are likely to recognize the word *long,* but as was discussed in Chapter 3 because the *g* is followed by the letter *i* it has the soft sound /j/. Table 5.1 provides other examples of words that may cause confusion. In these instances it would be better to direct students to decode the word using structural analysis or syllable types, as discussed in the following sections.

Table 5.1. Words That May Cause Confusion When Using the "Identify Known Parts" Strategy

Word	Recognizable Part
Signature	Sign
Monarch	Arch
Massacre	Acre
Spinal	Spin
Linear	Line
Molecule	Mole
Mineral	Mine
Ballot	Ball

Structural Analysis

Another strategy that may be helpful to introduce to students is to examine words for smaller meaningful parts, referred to as "structural analysis" (Nagy, Winsor, Osborn, & O'Flahavan, 1994). The basis of this strategy is to identify the morphemes that make up multisyllabic words. *Morphemes* are the smallest parts of words that have distinct meaning. There are two types of morphemes: free morphemes and bound morphemes. Free morphemes can stand alone as words without any other morphemes (e.g., *send, write, graph*). Bound morphemes must be attached to other morphemes. For example, the word *receive* is made up of two bound morphemes: *re* and *ceive*. Neither of these word parts can stand alone, but together they make a complete word. Generally, root words (e.g., *ceive*) and affixes (i.e., prefixes and suffixes) are bound morphemes while base words are free morphemes. Figure 5.1 illustrates the types of morphemes.

A benefit of structural analysis is that it helps students not only decode words but also determine their meaning. To teach this strategy effectively, you will need to teach students to recognize common prefixes and suffixes and their meanings. This strategy has high utility, as the four most common prefixes account for 58% of prefixed words in English, while the four most common suffixes account for 72% of suffixed words in English (Honig et al., 2000). These affixes can be found in Table 5.2. Because these affixes are so common, it is critical that students know them well.

The suffix *-ed* warrants particular attention because it has three sounds: /ed/ /d/ /t/ as shown in Table 5.3.

Figure 5.1. Types of Morphemes

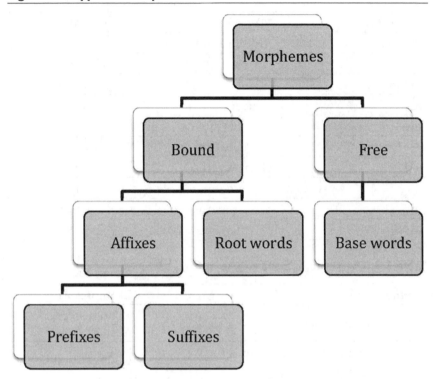

In later chapters, we will look more closely at affixes that are associated with particular content areas and how to use them to our advantage when teaching word meanings as part of word study instruction.

A research-based strategy that has been found to be effective in helping adolescents decode multisyllabic words through structural analysis is called the Word Identification Strategy and uses the acronym DISSECT, which stands for Discover the context, Isolate the prefix, Separate the suffix, Say the stem, Examine the stem, Check with someone, and Try the dictionary (Lenz & Hughes, 1990). This strategy helps students "dissect" large words and then decode the resulting smaller parts.

In Step 1 you would instruct students to read to the end of the sentence and use context to see if that helps them determine the unknown word. If after completing the first step students still do not know the word, you would guide them through Steps 2 through 5. In Step 2 you would teach students to isolate the prefix, and in Step 3 you would teach them how to separate the suffix. In Step 4 you would show them how to try and say the stem. If they do not know the stem, then you

Table 5.2. Most Common Prefixes and Suffixes

AFFIX	MEANING	EXAMPLE
	Prefixes	
dis-	opposite	disappear
in-, im-, il-, ir-	not	irreversible
re-	again	retry
un-	not	unfamiliar
	Suffixes	
-ed	past tense verbs	scurried
-ing	verb form/present participle	investigating
-ly	characteristic of	quietly
-s, -es	more than one	pipettes

Table 5.3. The Three Sounds of the Suffix -ed

Sound	Rule	Examples
/ed/	follows *t* and *d*	charted, experimented
/t/	follows voiceless sounds *f, k, p, s, x, ch, th,* and *sh*	watched, graphed
/d/	follows voiced sounds *b, g, l, m, n, r, v, z, th,* and vowels	observed, factored

would help them move to Step 5 and use the "rules of twos and threes" to determine the stem (Lenz, Shumaker, Deshler, & Beals, 1984). In the rules of twos and threes, if a stem begins with:

- a vowel, divide off the first two letters,
- a consonant, divide off the first three letters.

Once students have decoded the stem, you would help them put all of the parts of the word together. If the word is still unknown, encourage them to check with someone or use the dictionary. Let's try with the chemistry term *concentration* and assume that Step 1, Discover the context, is not helpful, so proceed to Step 2. In Step 2 instruct students to isolate the prefix *con* to make **con** centration. Then help students separate the suffix *tion* to make con centra **tion.** Next, ask students to say the stem *centra* as in con **centra** tion. Finally, have students examine the stem. In this case the stem *centra* begins with a consonant so students should divide off the first three letters as follows: con **cen/ tra** tion. Figure 5.2 provides additional examples of the DISSECT strategy.

Identifying Syllable Types

In English there are six syllable types. Multisyllabic words are essentially words made up of various combinations of these six different syllable types. Knowing the different syllable types and how to identify them in words is another strategy to help students decode multisyllabic words.

Before teaching students the six syllable types, they must first learn the meaning of a syllable. A *syllable* is a word or part of a word that has a spoken vowel sound with or without surrounding consonants. It is the presence of a vowel sound that turns a string of consonants into a word. This explains why *cll* is not a word but *cell* is. By counting the number of single vowels or vowel combinations, students can determine the number of syllables contained in a word. For example, there are five syllables in the word *thermodynamic*, three syllables in *exponent*, and one syllable in *moon*. Students may ask why *moon* only has one syllable when there are two vowels. The answer is because the two *o*'s in *moon* are functioning as a vowel digraph and only make one sound. Teaching students how to count the number of syllables in words will come in handy later when teaching them how to divide words.

After teaching students what syllables are and how to identify them, teachers can introduce the six syllable types:

1. **Closed syllable.** The most basic syllable has one vowel followed, and often preceded, by one or more consonants, and the vowel sound is short. The consonant-vowel-consonant (CVC) word *lab* is an example, as is a vowel consonant (VC) word like *at*. Be careful because there are some exceptions to the closed syllable including: *old, olt, oll, ost, olk, ild, ind, igh*.
2. **Open syllable.** This type of syllable ends with one vowel, and the vowel sound is long. The word *me* is an open syllable, while the prefix *re-* is also an open syllable.
3. **R-controlled syllable.** This type has a vowel followed by the letter *r*. The vowel and the letter *r* make one sound. *March, fort, twirl,* and *turn* are all words with r-controlled syllables.
4. **Vowel combination syllable.** This type has two vowels that occur together. The vowel sound can be long as in *meet*, short as in *bread*, or a dipthong as in *toy*.
5. **Vowel-consonant-e syllable.** This type of syllable is sometimes referred to as the "silent *e* rule." This syllable has a vowel

followed by a consonant followed by a silent letter *e*, and the vowel sound is long. *Note*, *hide*, and *name* are a few examples.

6. **Consonant-le syllable**. This is an ending syllable that has a consonant followed by *le* as in *subtle* or *humble*.

Once students know the syllable types, they can look for them in unknown words and have a better way to predict how the word is broken apart and what the vowel sounds will be. For example, look at the word *explorer*. There are three syllables in this word. We can tell because there are three separate vowels. The three syllables are closed,

Figure 5.2. Examples of the DISSECT Strategy

Example 1- *transcontinental*

Step 1: Using the sentence context did not help
Step 2: Isolate the Prefix   **trans** continental
Step 3: Separate the Suffix   trans continent **al**
Step 4: Say the stem   trans **continent** al
Step 5: Examine stem using rules of twos and threes
trans **con/ tinent** al
stem begins with consonant so divide off first three letters

trans + con/ tinent + al = *transcontinental*
Example 2- *refraction*

Step 1: Using the sentence context did not help.
Step 2: Isolate the Prefix   **re** fraction
Step 3: Separate the Suffix   re frac **tion**
Step 4: Say the stem   re **frac** tion
Step 5: Examine stem using rules of twos and threes
re **frac** tion
not necessary because stem is only one syllable

re + frac + tion = *refraction*
Example 3- *subcontractor*

Step 1: Using the sentence context did not help.
Step 2: Isolate the Prefix   **sub** contractor
Step 3: Separate the Suffix   sub contract **or**
Step 4: Say the stem   sub **contract** or
Step 5: Examine stem using rules of twos and threes
sub **con / tract** or
stem begins with consonant so divide off first three letters
sub + con / tract + or = *subcontractor*

r-controlled, and r-controlled: Ex/plor/er. Table 5.4 provides some examples of the six syllable types in multisyllabic words.

Division Patterns

While some students may be able to identify the syllable types in words simply by looking for them in multisyllabic words as we did with the word *explorer* above, others may need more support. Teaching students several division patterns and helping them apply these patterns to unknown words can help them in their reading. Be aware that helping students become proficient in using division patterns will require an initial investment of instructional time. Students will need to be explicitly taught the division patterns and then given multiple opportunities to practice under your guidance before trying to apply the division patterns independently. If you are like many secondary teachers I know, the thought of taking time away from the vast amount of content you are expected to teach will seem ludicrous. However, consider for a moment the amount of extra instructional time you might have later if you do not have to repeatedly respond to students' need for help decoding unfamiliar words. Think also about how students' confidence, motivation, and engagement could be increased if they had tools that helped them overcome some of their reading challenges. The initial investment will pay dividends in the long term. If you are still unsure whether you can devote time to this instruction, it may be worthwhile to collaborate with a reading coach or specialist. The reading specialist could teach the division patterns up front, and then you could help students practice when unfamiliar words present themselves in class.

Teaching the division patterns does not have to interfere with your need to spend the majority of instructional time teaching your particular content area. One possibility is to introduce one division pattern a

Table 5.4. Six Syllable Types with Multisyllabic Examples

Syllable Type	Examples of Multisyllabic Words
Closed	manhunt, pumpkin, administration
Open	triangle, rerun, bacon
R-controlled	forlorn, barber, perpendicular
Vowel combinations	maintain, railroad, indeed, proofread
Vowel-consonant-*e*	contrive, decide, demote, microphone
Consonant-*le*	paddle, beetle, trouble, invisible

week during the first or last five minutes of class. Within 5 weeks you will have taught all of the patterns. Once you have initially taught the division patterns explicitly with ample opportunities to practice, it will only be necessary to ensure students have ongoing opportunities to review the division patterns so they do not forget and to provide error correction if students make mistakes.

The first step in using division patterns is to teach students to mark the consonants in words with a *c* and the vowels with a *v*. Let's try with the word *fragment*:

c	c	v	c	c	v	c	c
f	r	a	g	m	e	n	t

Next teach students to look for specific patterns that will indicate where to divide the word into smaller parts. The first pattern is VCCV. When students see two consonants between two vowels they should be directed to divide between the consonants:

c	c	v	c	c	v	c	c
f	r	a	g	m	e	n	t

Now students can see that the word *fragment* is made up of two closed syllables: *frag* and *ment*. When using division patterns students must also be taught to keep consonant blends (e.g., *sm-, -mp*) consonant digraphs (e.g., *ch, th*), vowel digraphs (e.g., *ee, ou*) and vowel dipthongs (e.g., *oi, oy*) together. For example, look at the word *humpback:*

c	v	c	c	c	v	c	c
h	u	m	p	b	a	c	k

In this word we see the pattern VCCCV and so students may be confused about where to divide. We remind them that blends and digraphs stay together and act as one unit as shown below.

c	v	c	c	c	v	c	c
h	u	m	p	b	a	c	k

The next division pattern is VCV, or one consonant between two vowels. In this instance, students should divide between the first vowel and the consonant. Try it with the word *preside*.

c	c	v	c	v	c	v
p	r	e	s	i	d	e

Now students should be able to see an open syllable *pre* and vowel-consonant-*e* syllable *side*. If you look closely, you will see a second VCV combination (*ide*). So why not divide after the letter *i*? The answer is because the *e* is silent according to the vowel-consonant-*e* syllable rule. So therefore, it is not acting like a true vowel does in a syllable. It is helpful to teach students to immediately identify any vowel-consonant-*e* syllables and draw a line through the letter *e* as opposed to marking it with a v:

c	v	c	c	v	c	
c	o	n	c	e	d	ҽ̸

Because vowels can function in different ways in words, sometimes dividing after the first vowel will be incorrect. Take the word *Spanish*. If students apply our VCV pattern and divide between the first vowel and consonant it would look like this:

c	c	v	c	v	c	c
S	p	a	n	i	s	h

This creates the open syllable *Spa* and the closed syllable *nish*. But to be correct, the *a* in *Spanish* needs to have the short sound rather than the long sound. This brings us to the second part of the VCV division pattern, which is to tell students to divide after the consonant. When we apply this pattern to *Spanish*, we get:

c	c	v	c	v	c	c
S	p	a	n	i	s	h

Closed syllable *Span* and closed syllable *ish* = Spanish.
The next division pattern is a little tricky because it occurs when

two vowels are together but they are not functioning as a vowel combination syllable. Instead, each vowel is functioning as a syllable, as in the word *neon*. *Neon* has two syllables: open syllable *ne* and closed syllable *on*. For these words the pattern is VV and students should divide between the two vowels, as in this example:

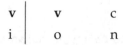

Luckily, there are not many words with this pattern, but it is a useful strategy for students to keep in the back of their minds.

The last division pattern is used with consonant-*le* syllables. This one is fairly easy for students to learn and apply. The division pattern is to divide before the consonant-*le*. So the word *marble* would have two syllables: *mar* and *ble*.

Putting all of the information about division patterns together with respect to the word *microphone* would look like this:

1. Underline any letter combinations (digraphs, blends, dipthongs).

   m   i   <u>cr</u>   o   <u>ph</u>   o   n   e

2. Cross out the silent *e* if there is one.

   m   i   <u>cr</u>   o   <u>ph</u>   o   n   ~~e~~

3. Mark the vowels and consonants.

c	v	c	v	c	v	c	
m	i	<u>cr</u>	o	<u>ph</u>	o	n	~~e~~

4. Look for recognizable division patterns.

c	v		c	v		c	v	c	
m	i		<u>cr</u>	o		<u>ph</u>	o	n	~~e~~

5. Say the individual parts.

   mi cro phone

6. Say the parts together fast.

   microphone

7. Is it a real word?

   Yes!

If the answer to number 7 is no, instruct students to go back and try applying different division rules or trying different vowel sounds. Also keep in mind the context. Does it sound close to a real word that is being used in that particular context? For example, if students are learning about minerals in their science class and they decode the word *mineral* as mine/ral, prompt them to ask whether this word sounds like any words they have been discussing in science. (A reproducible sheet with the above script can be downloaded for free at www.tcpress.com.) If students are reading out of a textbook or library book in which they should not write, have them keep a piece of scratch paper and pencil nearby so they can quickly write down the word and then mark the consonants and vowels and draw the division lines. You can also give students small Post-it notes to affix directly above an unknown word, where they can then mark the consonants and vowels. The following paragraph shows how a teacher might incorporate the division patterns into instruction.

> Mr. Ming and the students in his English/language arts class are reading the novel *Hound of the Baskervilles* by Arthur Conan Doyle. Today, students will read a passage containing the following sentence: "It is not my intention to be fulsome, but I confess that I covet your skull." Mr. Ming plans to use this sentence as a practice opportunity for students to apply their knowledge of the division patterns. He writes the sentence on the board and underlines the following words: *intention, fulsome,* and *confess*. He directs students to take out their English/L.A. notebooks and turn to the vocabulary section in which they keep a running list of target vocabulary words and notes about the division patterns. Mr. Ming asks students to write down the three underlined words and then divide them by marking the consonants and vowels. When the class is finished, he calls three volunteers up to the board to model for the rest of the class. The three volunteers correctly divide the word using the VCCV division pattern:

v	c	c	v	c	c	v	v	c
i	n	t	e	n	t	i	o	n

c	v	c	c	v	c
f	u	l	s	o	m	e

c	v	c	c	v	c	c
c	o	n	f	e	s	s

He thanks the volunteers and asks students in the class to turn to a partner and take turns reading the words. The last word Mr. Ming wants to discuss is *covet*. Mr. Ming knows that most of his students will be unfamiliar with this word. If students apply the traditional division patterns they will most likely find the VCV pattern and divide after the first vowel. This, however, results in the open syllable *co* and closed syllable *vet*, but this is incorrect as shown below.

c	v	c	v	c
c	o	v	e	t

Instead, Mr. Ming tells students this word is a little tricky and then proceeds to explicitly guide students through the proper division so the result is the closed syllable *cov* and closed syllable *et*. In total, it takes about 7 minutes for Mr. Ming and his students to divide the four words. With this upfront practice opportunity, Mr. Ming feels more confident that his students will use the division patterns as needed when they read the next chapter in the novel.

The Schwa Sound

When discussing how to decode multisyllabic words, there is a sound that warrants particular attention. The *schwa sound* is "the neutral vowel in unaccented or unstressed syllables in English words, such as the sound that corresponds to the grapheme *a* in *asleep*" (Henry, 2003, p. 289). Some words with the schwa sound are: *about, atlas, banana, carrot, curious, enemy, mountain, other, problem.* If students are attempting to decode a word and neither the short nor long vowel sounds work, direct them to try the schwa sound.

SPELLING INSTRUCTION

Up to this point we have only discussed strategies to help students decode multisyllabic words, but word study is more than just reading words. To succeed in secondary classrooms, students must also be able to *spell* (or *encode*) words correctly. Word study helps students become better spellers because students can use their knowledge of how to spell individual word parts to form longer multisyllabic words.

Spelling instruction should not be an afterthought. Decoding and encoding (spelling) share a common system of patterns (Henry, 2003); by teaching spelling rules and patterns, teachers are reinforcing comparable decoding skills. Ultimately, spelling instruction is important because it actually helps students become better decoders and readers (Moats, 2005). I was recently observing a middle school language arts classroom in which a student was reading aloud from a novel. He encountered the sentence, "She peered into the *gaping* hole." The student read the sentence as, "She peered into the *gapping* hole." Then he looked up in confusion. Here is an example in which having some basic knowledge of spelling rules can help students be better decoders. Knowing that when adding the suffix *-ing* to a vowel-consonant-*e* word the letter *e* is dropped but the vowel retains the long sound would have helped this student decode *gaping* correctly: gape + ing = gaping.

The key with spelling instruction is to address students' errors as soon as possible (Wanzek et al., 2006). Instead of just telling students the correct spelling, it is more effective to teach or review the relevant spelling rule(s) (Simonsen & Gunter, 2001). The following spelling rules not only help support students' decoding, but they are also commonly applied when spelling multisyllabic words.

Doubling Rule

The doubling rule specifies that when you add a suffix that begins with a vowel to a one-syllable word that ends with one vowel followed by one consonant (VC), the final consonant should be doubled. For example, *run* becomes *running*. Here *run* is a one-syllable word that ends in the VC pattern, and we are adding the suffix *-ing* which begins with a vowel. Hence, the letter *n* in *run* should be doubled. Notable exceptions are words that end in the letters *y* or *w*, as in the words *play* or *plow*. *Play* + *ing* becomes *playing* (not *playyying*) and *plow* + *ed* is *plowed* (not *plowwed*). This is because the *y* and *w* are acting as vowels or vowel combinations and therefore do not follow the VC pattern. Final consonants are also doubled in multisyllabic words in which the final syllable has the VC pattern and is stressed or accented like in the word *prefer*. Adding the suffix *-ed* to *prefer* results in the word *preferred*. When the VC pattern is not stressed in a final syllable, the final consonant is not doubled as in *traveling* or *benefiting*.

Changing *y* to *i* Rule

The changing *y* to *i* rule applies to words that end in the letter *y*. When making such words plural, sometimes you need to change the *y* to the letter *i* before adding the suffix *-es*. Other times the *y* remains and you simply add the suffix *-s*. The key to determining whether to keep the *y* or change it to *i* is based on what type of letter—vowel or consonant—directly precedes the letter *y*. If a vowel comes before the *y* as in *deploy*, simply add the suffix *-s* to make *deploys*. If, on the other hand, a consonant precedes the *y* as in the word *body*, then it is necessary to change the *y* to *i* before adding the suffix *-es*. *Body* becomes *bodies*.

Although this rule is often thought about only when making nouns plural or verbs third person singular, it also applies to other suffixes like *-ed*, used to make verbs past tense, and *-er* and *-est*, typically used with adjectives and adverbs. The same rules for changing the *y* to *i* apply when adding these other suffixes. Note that there are very few adjectives or adverbs that end with a vowel followed by the letter *-y*. See Figure 5.3 for examples of the changing *y* to *i* rule.

Changing *f* Rule

The changing *f* rule applies to words that end in *f* or *fe* and are being made plural. In these instances the letter *f* is changed to the letter *v* before adding the suffix *-es*. For example, *wife* becomes *wives* and *loaf* becomes *loaves*. Of course, there are some exceptions, usually found in words that end in *ff* or *ief*, such as *cuff* and *belief*. Simply add the suffix *-s* to these words: the plural of *cuff* is *cuffs* and *belief* is *beliefs*.

Final *e* Rule

The final *e* rule stipulates that when adding a suffix that begins with a vowel to a word that ends in *e*, the *e* is dropped before adding the suffix as in the following examples:

Figure 5.3. Examples of the Changing y to *i* Rule

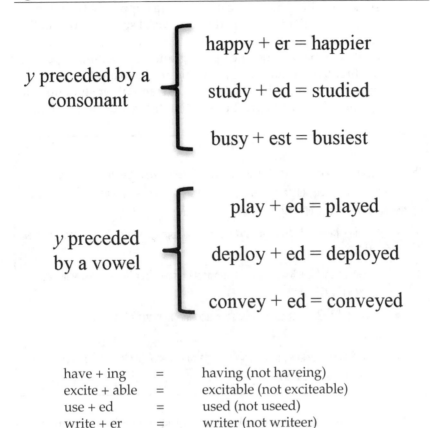

y preceded by a consonant

- happy + er = happier
- study + ed = studied
- busy + est = busiest

y preceded by a vowel

- play + ed = played
- deploy + ed = deployed
- convey + ed = conveyed

have + ing	=	having (not haveing)
excite + able	=	excitable (not exciteable)
use + ed	=	used (not useed)
write + er	=	writer (not writeer)
brave + est	=	bravest (not braveest)

Exceptions include adding -*able* to words that end in -*ce* or -*ge*. For example, manage + able = *manageable* and notice + able = *noticeable*.

Technology and Spelling

For older struggling readers and students with disabilities, technology-based applications provide many opportunities for spelling practice and support. Here is one example of how a teacher incorporates technology-based spelling practice into her classroom:

> Ms. Wilde teaches U.S. Government to high school students. One of her students, Claire, has a reading disability and struggles with spelling, especially the multisyllabic words commonly used in class like *legislative, judicial, executive,* and

constitutional. To provide Claire (and other students with similar spelling difficulties) with extra support, Ms. Wilde keeps some iPads equipped with several spelling apps in the classroom. Each week Ms. Wilde inputs the key terms students will be reading and spelling into the spelling apps. For the first five minutes of class while students are turning in homework and getting settled, Claire and other students with spelling difficulties practice spelling the words on the iPads.

TECH TIP

There are several great (and free) apps to help students with spelling. Designed for smartphones and tablets, these apps allow students to practice spelling while they are on the go and without drawing attention to themselves.

- Spelling Notebook Free. https://itunes.apple.com/us/app/spelling-notebook-free/id461225509?mt=8

- Speaking Spelling Bee. https://itunes.apple.com/us/app/speaking-spelling-bee/id386617292?mt=8

- Miss Spell's Class. http://www.macworld.com/product/67043/miss-spell-s-class.html

- Skill Builder Spelling. https://play.google.com/store/apps/details?id=com.kaiserapps.skillbuilderspelling&hl=en

---

I often encounter people who say that spelling instruction is obsolete because of new technologies and programs like Spellcheck and Speech-to-Text software. There is no doubt that these tools make spelling easier, but there is still a place for spelling instruction. For one thing, spell-check programs are not entirely accurate and do not take into account the sentence context (Montgomery, Karlan, & Coutinho, 2001). Such is the case when spell-checkers do not alert you that you have used *their* when you should have used *there*.

To take full advantage of spelling assistance programs, students must be able to approximate words so that spell-checkers can recognize the attempted word. For example, when I spelled *route* as *rowt*, my spell-checker's suggestions were: *row, rot, rows, rout,* and *root*, none of which were correct. Whether spell-check programs produce the correct word is also dependent on whether students can correctly spell the first letter or combination of letters. When I spelled the word *financial* as *phinancial* my spell-checker could not recognize the word and had

© Randy Glasbergen / glasbergen.com

**"My report is about music from the 1960's,
but my spell-checker made me leave out
The Beatles, Monkees, and Byrds!"**

"no spelling suggestions." This discussion is particularly relevant for students with disabilities, inasmuch as research has shown that the misspellings of students with learning disabilities are not close approximations of the target word (Montgomery et al., 2001).

Students also have to be familiar enough with a word's correct spelling to be able to pick it out from among other visually similar options. For example, when I spelled the word *arraignment* as *araingement*, among my spell-checker options were *arrangement* and *arraignment*—options that might be too close for some students to differentiate and then pick the correct choice.

Speech-to-text and dictation software programs seem to be slightly more accurate and reliable, provided the speaker dictates clearly, slowly, and without a noticeable accent or dialectal difference. Despite my repeated attempts, however, dictating *Tyrannosaurus rex* always came out as *to rent a source Rex*. If you are interested in trying some of these types of programs in your classroom check out the Tech Tip for resources.

Teaching students strategies to decode and spell multisyllabic words using their knowledge of known parts or the syllable types will provide them with tools with which to tackle the many multisyllabic words found in content area texts. With this knowledge students may be less likely to skip or gloss over words that would otherwise seem too challenging. Students may also be more motivated to read because they experience greater success without relying on adult assistance.

TECH TIP

The following apps are great resources and supports for students who have reading and writing difficulties or disabilities.

- Speak it! Text to Speech by Future Apps Inc. https://itunes.apple.com/us/app/speak-it!-text-to-speech/id308629295?mt=8

- Dragon Dictation by Nuance Communications. http://www.nuance.com/for-individuals/mobile-applications/dragon-dictation/index.htm

- Typ-O HD Writing Is for Everybody! by SecondGuess ApS. https://itunes.apple.com/us/app/typ-o-hd-writing-is-for-everybody!/id372971659?mt=8

DISCUSSION QUESTIONS

1. Do any students in your classes still need basic word study instruction? If yes, who provides this instruction? How does this instruction fit into students' school day?

2. What challenges do you see the adolescents with disabilities in your class encounter regarding multisyllabic decoding? Which strategies for decoding unknown words will be the easiest for you to implement in your classroom?

3. Recall a time when you were confronted with text that you could not easily decode. Maybe it was when you were learning a foreign language or reading a textbook in a content area that was new to you. How did it feel? What did you learn from this experience?

4. What do the students with disabilities in your class do when they encounter an unknown multisyllabic word? Do they skip it? Do they substitute a word that starts with the same first letter or one that looks similar? Do they mumble through it hoping nobody notices their difficulties? Do they pause hoping that you or one of their classmates will immediately provide the correct word? If you are not sure, take some time to have students read aloud to you and make notes about what strategies they are (or are not) using.

5. What challenges do you see the adolescents with disabilities in your class encounter regarding spelling? Can their spelling errors provide insights into their decoding abilities or difficulties?

Part III

WORD STUDY IN SECONDARY CLASSROOMS

CHAPTER 6

Word Study at Work in the Content Area Classroom

Although the general rules and recommendations of advanced word study presented in Chapter 5 can be applied in any content area classroom, there are differences and trends across specific disciplines that warrant focused explanation and discussion. In this chapter I explore the language foundations upon which particular disciplines are based. I also explore the particular linguistic features of various disciplines that make reading and understanding multisyllabic words difficult for struggling readers and students with disabilities.

MATHEMATICS

Wait! If this book is all about reading, why is mathematics included?

It is true the bulk of mathematical language and notation is comprised of numerals and symbols. However, being able to decode and understand mathematical terminology and vocabulary is critical for student success. Look at the following sentences that might be found in geometry and algebra textbooks:

1. Tell whether the line or segment is best described as a chord, a secant, a tangent, a diameter, or a radius of circle C.
2. Use the distributive property to find the value of each expression.

In these questions, being able to read the key terms and understand what they mean is necessary for students to successfully complete the problems. This is difficult for students with disabilities who struggle in reading because math texts tend to be dense, compact, and contain multiple concepts within a single sentence (Kenney et al., 2005).

Mathematics word problems can be challenging for all students and in particular struggling readers and students with disabilities

(Cirino, Fuchs, Tolar, & Powell, 2011). For example, read this geometry problem:

> A circular disc is placed on the ground. It is then rotated 310 degrees in a clockwise direction so that a red arrow that has been drawn on the disc points north. The same result would have occurred if the disc had instead been rotated _____.

In this mathematics word problem there is only one number, but students must be able to decode and understand the meaning of words like *circular, rotated, clockwise,* and *direction*. If students spend all of their cognitive effort decoding and understanding the key words, they will have little energy left to solve conceptually challenging, multicomponent word problems.

To make matters more complicated for students, whether they have disabilities or not, some mathematical terms have multiple meanings (Kenney et al., 2005). For example, the words *expression, operation, term,* and *property* have specific meanings in mathematics that differ from their meanings in general daily use. Even if students can decode such words, they may struggle to understand them in the context of mathematics. Here is a list of other mathematics terms that have multiple meanings: *chord, constant, degree, error, factor, identity, intersection, mean, plane, power, proof, rational, rise, run, series, set.*

In mathematics, some affixes are more common than others. Prefixes that denote quantities like *uni-, bi-, tri-, poly-,* and *multi-* are

**"No, I can't explain my D in math. That class
teaches us about numbers, not letters!"**

common across mathematics content, as in the words *triangle, binomial, unilateral, polygon,* and *multivariate.* Table 6.1 provides a list of common prefixes in mathematics.

The following paragraph shows how a teacher might incorporate word study into a mathematics class.

> Mr. Abrams and the students in his geometry class are learning about polygons, so he uses this opportunity to teach students the prefix *poly-* as he knows this word part will appear in other mathematics and science classes. He tells students *poly-* means many. Then he has them write it down in their geometry notebooks. He continues by stating the definition of a *polygon* as a closed plane figure with many (i.e., at least three) straight sides. Students write this definition in their notebooks and then draw a series of shapes that represent examples and nonexamples.

SCIENCE

The language of science has its foundations in Greek (Henry, 2003). Recall from Chapter 3 that American English is derived from Anglo-Saxon, Greek, and Latin. Greek contributions, particularly in the area of science, include combining forms. *Combining forms* are "word parts of Greek origin that can be combined with other combining forms or morphemes to form new words" (Henry, 2003, p. 286). For example, you can combine the words *photo* and *graph* to create the new concept *photograph.* Similarly, you can combine the prefix *micro* to the root *scope* to get the name of the instrument *microscope.* Or you can combine the prefix *psych-* with the root *ology* to get the science of *psychology.* See Table 6.2 for a list of Greek combining forms.

Also from Greek come three letter–sound correspondences that students will need to be explicitly taught, as they are common but nonphonetic. First, the grapheme *ph* makes the /f/ sound as in *photo* and *physiology.* Second, the grapheme *ch* makes the /k/ sound as in *chemical* and *psychiatry.* Finally, the letter *y* can make the short /i/ sound as in *system,* but it can also make the long /i/ sound as in *hypothermia.* There are also several letter–sound correspondences that are nonphonetic but less common, such as *pn* in *pneumonia* and *pt* in *pterodactyl.* In general, the first letter is silent in these letter–sound correspondences (see Table 6.3).

Table 6.1. Prefixes Commonly Used in Mathematics

Prefix	Meaning	Example
uni-	one	univariate
bi-	two	bilateral
di-	two	diameter
tri-	three	triangle
quad-	four	quadruple
ex-	out, upwards	exponent
equi-	equal	equidistant
milli-	one-thousandth	millimeter
centi-	one-hundredth	centiliter
deci-	one-tenth	decigram
kilo-	thousand	kilometer

Table 6.2. Common Combining Forms from Greek

Combining Form	Meaning	Example
geo	earth	geothermal
gram, graph	written or drawn	diagram
hydr, hydra, hydro,	water	hydrate
micro	small	microbe
ology	study of	psychology
photo	light	photograph
phys	nature	physical
scope	watch or see	telescope
techn, techno	skill	technology
tele	distant	television
therm, thermo	heat	thermal

Here is a vignette that illustrates how one teacher incorporates technology-supported writing instruction in her science class.

> Mrs. Ortiz's physics students have just completed a lab on acceleration. Students worked in pairs to measure each other's running speed using a motion detector. Now students are ready to write their results in a lab report. Mrs. Ortiz checked

Table 6.3. Nonphonetic Letter-Sound Correspondences from Greek

Grapheme	Phoneme	Example
mn	/n/	mnemonic
pn	/n/	pneumonia
ps	/s/	psychology
pt	/t/	pterodactyl
rh	/r/	rhinoceros

out the school's mobile laptop cart so students have their own laptop to use in writing their lab reports. On three laptops Mrs. Ortiz has installed the CAST Science Writer software program so the students with disabilities in the class have extra support. This program provides a series of supports designed to benefit students with disabilities. The program has a science report template that breaks writing tasks down into smaller chunks, sentence starters, text-to-speech capability, and a journal feature where students can record their notes. Toward the end of the class period Mrs. Ortiz checks on the students with disabilities and notices two are misspelling some key vocabulary terms. Both students misspell *velocity* as "velosity" and *acceleration* as "acseleration." Mrs. Ortiz makes a note to provide these students with a brief minilesson on the soft *c* sound at the start of class the next day.

TECH TIP

These software programs provide writing support for struggling writers. The CAST Science Writer provides specific support for writing science reports.

- Kurzweil 3000: www.kurzweiledu.com/default.html
- CAST Science Writer: sciencewriter.cast.org/welcome;jsessionid= 45AB8D9083AE6CEC9155B1DCC78714E9

ENGLISH/LANGUAGE ARTS AND SOCIAL STUDIES

Within English/language arts and social studies, many key words originated from Latin. Latin roots can be combined with prefixes and suffixes to create words: *trans-*+ port+-*ed* = *transported*; re-+flect=

Table 6.4. Common Latin Roots

Root	Meaning	Example
capit, capt	head or chief	capitol
cap, ceit, ceive, cep, cep, cept, cip	take, catch, seize, hold, receive	receive
cede, ceed, cess	go, yield, surrender	proceed
cise	cut	excise
cred	believe	credible
dic, dict	say or tell	dictation
fac, fact, fect, fir	make or do	confection
feder, fid, fide, feal	trust or faith	confederation
fer	bear or yield	transfer
flect, flex	bend or curve	deflect
form	shape	forming
jac, jec, ject	throw or lie	object
lect, leg, lig	choose, pick, read, or speak	lecture
mit, miss	end	dismiss
port	carry	export
pend, pens	hang or weigh	suspend
pon, pose, pound	put, place, set	compound
rupt	break or burst	erupt
scrib, script	write	inscription
sist, sta, stat, stit	stand	institute
spe, spect, spic	see, watch, observe	spectator
stru, struct	build	destruction
ten, tain, tin, tinu	hold	obtain
tend, tens, tent	stretch or strain	attention
vers, vert	turn	reverse
vid, vis	see	visible
vit, vita, viv, vivi	live	vitality

reflect; centi-+ ped+-es= *centipedes*. Table 6.4 provides a list of Latin roots.

When combining Latin roots and affixes there are some guidelines to keep in mind. In most cases, the Latin root is phonetic as in *rupt*, *cred*, and *tend*. Roots can have two or more forms as *stru* and *struct* or *duc*, *duce*, and *duct* (Henry, 2003). When combining some roots and suffixes, a "connective" is required (Henry, 2003). *Connectives—i, u, ul*—literally connect the root to the suffix. Combining *apt* with *tude* requires the connective *i* = *aptitude*. The connectives *u* and *ul* are always long vowel sounds as in *monument* and *muscular*. The connective *i* makes three different sounds depending on what letter precedes or follows it: (1) Before a vowel suffix, *i* takes the long /e/ sound: *memorial*; (2) before a consonant suffix, *i* takes the short /i/ sound: *multitude*; (3) following *l* or *n*, *i* takes the /y/ sound: *billion*.

There are some suffixes that warrant direct teaching because they are nonphonetic (see Table 6.5).

When combining Latin roots and affixes to make multisyllabic words, the vowel sounds may shift. For example, in the word *munici-pal* the letter *a* makes the schwa sound, but in the word *municipality* the letter *a* makes the short /a/ sound.

The following vignette shows word study in action in a social studies classroom.

> Ms. Reynolds wants students in her Word History course to review vocabulary that is a part of their unit on the Middle Ages. Ms. Reynolds writes several vocabulary terms on the board including: *conqueror, invasion, knighthood, jousting, archbishop, monarchy*, and *serfdom*. Before asking students to complete a crossword puzzle with these terms and their meanings, Ms. Reynolds wants to draw students' attention to the various affixes contained in the vocabulary terms. She asks the students to write down the words and then circle any prefixes and underline any suffixes. She models the correct answers on the board so students can check their work. Then Ms. Reynolds and the students have a brief discussion in which they review the function of affixes and how they change the meanings of base and root words.

BUT WHAT DOES IT ALL MEAN?

Word study is not only about correctly decoding and spelling words, but it also involves determining the meaning of words. This is where vocabulary instruction comes into play. Providing vocabulary instruction and strategies that will help struggling readers and students with disabilities understand multisyllabic words is a critical component in their success in reading (Beck, McKeown, & Kucan, 2002; Boardman et al., 2008) and content area classes. Beck and colleagues (2002)

Table 6.5. Nonphonetic Letter–Sound Correspondences in Suffixes

Grapheme	Phoneme	Example
ci	/sh/	glacial
cian	/shun/	pediatrician
ti	/sh/	partial
tion	/shun/	nation
tu	/choo/	mutual
ture	/cher/	temperature

recommend robust vocabulary instruction—vocabulary instruction that moves beyond rudimentary definition drills to include learning opportunities that make use of authentic experiences and texts across varied contexts (NRP, 2000). The goal of robust vocabulary instruction is not simply for students to memorize basic definitions, but also to develop a deep working knowledge of words that includes their definition, their relationship to other words, and how they operate in different contexts (Stahl & Kapinus, 2001).

Before we discuss *how* to provide robust vocabulary instruction within word study, we must first determine *which* words to teach. As I suggested earlier in the book, there is not enough time to directly teach every new vocabulary term students will encounter in a content area class (Diamond & Gutlohn, 2006). Research has shown that between 8 and 10 new words or root words can be realistically taught a week (Beck et al., 2002; Biemiller, 2005). It is also important to dedicate time each week to reviewing previously learned words (Beck et al., 2002). Selecting only 10 words per week to teach from hundreds of potential words will be difficult, so here are a few tips:

1. Identify the most important words within a particular lesson, experience, or unit. In a lesson on the branches of government, directly teaching the words *executive, judicial,* and *legislative* is probably a good use of vocabulary instructional time.
2. Identify words that have a high level of utility within content areas. The word *experiment* appears in many fields within science. Making sure students know this term will serve them well in their current and future science classes.
3. Identify words that are used across content areas. The word *equation* is used in mathematics and science, while *precipitation* is discussed in social studies and science.

Structural Analysis

Structural analysis is the process of using affixes, root words, and base words to determine the meaning of words (Nagy et al., 1994). This process is also referred to as "morphemic analysis" because affixes, root words, and base words are all morphemes, or meaning-based parts of words (Diamond & Gutlohn, 2006). Spending time teaching word learning via structural analysis will provide struggling readers and students with disabilities with a concrete approach to decoding and understanding unfamiliar words. In fact, structural analysis provides word-learning tools that can benefit *all* students. This is good news because taken together, Greek combining forms and Latin root words account for hundreds of thousands of words (Henry, 2003).

Your instructional time will be best spent if you identify the morphemes that either occur commonly within your content area or make up words that are critical to a lesson or unit.

Treat various morphemes according to the instructional principles introduced in Chapter 4 (i.e., explicit, systematic instruction with plentiful opportunities to practice with immediate feedback). Students should memorize how to decode them *and* what they mean.

> *(Teacher writes* macro *on board.)*
>
> **Teacher:** This is the Greek combining form *macro*. When we add *macro* to the beginning of some words or word parts it changes their meaning. *Macro* means large. What does *macro* mean?
> **Students:** Large.
> **Teacher:** Yes, *macro* means large.
>
> *(Teacher writes the word* fossil *on board.)*
>
> **Teacher:** So when I add the prefix *macro* to the word *fossil* it makes the word *macrofossil*. Let's try it together. *Macro* + *fossil* makes what new word?
> **Students:** Macrofossil.
> **Teacher:** If the prefix *macro* means large, what does *macrofossil* mean?
> **Students:** Large fossil.
> **Teacher:** Yes, in fact macrofossils are fossils that are large enough to be seen without a microscope.

As students expand their morphemic vocabularies they can experiment with inferring the meaning of new words based on known parts. For example, if students know the Latin root *form* means to shape and the prefix *con* means with or together, they should be able to conclude that *conform* has something to do with shaping things so they are more similar. Likewise, if students know that *biology* means the study of living organisms and *microscopes* are used to examine very small objects, then they can make the educated guess that *microbiology* is the study of very small organisms.

When teaching structural analysis, it is wise to be on the lookout for imposters. Some words have "false" morphemes or parts of words that appear to be morphemes but actually are not (Henry, 2003). The word *uncle* begins with *un* but it is not a prefix in this case. Similarly, *reward* begins with *re* but not as a prefix. Students need to be aware of instances like these so they do not try to apply structural analysis methods inappropriately. Providing students with examples like the ones above is a good way to illustrate the idea of "imposters."

Graphic and Semantic Organizers

Graphic and semantic organizers are instructional tools that can be used to organize and visually represent information. Within word study, these tools are especially useful in helping students expand their word learning by manipulating word parts to form new and more complex words. Figures 6.1, 6.2, and 6.3 illustrate graphic organizers that can be used as part of a lesson in structural analysis. Once students have learned several affixes and base or root words, they can combine them to create root or base word families. Figure 6.1 displays a three-square graphic organizer that helps students create a base or root word family. In the figure, *struct* is written in the center. From here students can connect *struct* to one or two other squares to make a series of multisyllabic words with the root word *struct*, like *instruct, construction, destructed,* and so on.

It is possible that not all students will automatically know what graphic organizers are or how they can be used to help them learn the meanings of words. I recommend taking some instructional time to directly teach students how to properly use semantic and graphic organizers. Think back to the My Turn–Together–Your Turn teaching format from Chapter 4. I often start by showing students a blank organizer and then model how to complete it (My Turn). I use a think-aloud process in which I verbalize my thoughts as I complete the organizer.

(Teacher displays a blank version of Figure 6.3 graphic organizer)

Teacher: This is a graphic organizer that can help us organize words that share the same root word. Let me show you how it works with the root word *port.*

(Teacher writes port in the middle circle.)

Teacher: Remember we learned that *port* means to carry. I'm going to combine the root word *port* with some prefixes we have learned. Hmmm, let's add the prefix *im*.

(Teacher writes import *in one circle.)*

Teacher: We get *import*. Remember *im* means in. So *import* means to carry in.

(Teacher continues modeling with other prefixes until all circles are completed.)

Then, I would provide an opportunity for students to complete the same graphic organizer with a different root word in small groups or individually with my support and feedback as needed (Together). Finally, I would have students complete a graphic organizer individually (Your Turn). Once students are comfortable and proficient using a specific graphic or semantic organizer, the explicit instructional procedure presented above is no longer necessary. Providing a quick reminder or brief example of the graphic organizer should be sufficient to get students started.

Graphic organizers can be used to develop multiple words from the same root word as shown in Figures 6.1 and 6.2. Or graphic organizers can be used to help students apply structural analysis to decode and determine the meaning of unknown multisyllabic words. Figure 6.3 displays a graphic organizer that has been completed using the word *replacement*.

Whether you are a mathematics, science, English, or social studies teacher, teaching word study strategies that account for the unique linguistic features of your discipline will benefit all students in your classes. When students are able to be more independent decoders, spellers, and vocabulary meaning-makers, your instructional time and

Figure 6.1. Three-Square Graphic Organizer for Creating a Root Word Family

de	in	con
ing	**struct**	ure
ed	s	ion

Note: A blank reproducible version of this figure is available for free download at www. tcpress.com

Figure 6.2. Graphic Organizer for Words Sharing the Same Root Word

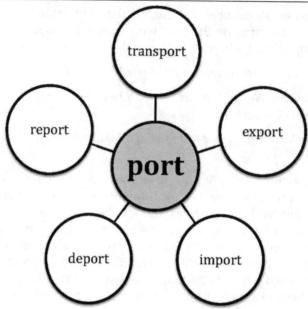

Note: A blank reproducible version of this figure is available for free download at www.tcpress.com

Figure 6.3. Graphic Organizer for Decoding a Word to Find Its Meaning

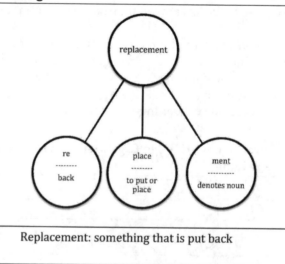

Note: A blank reproducible version of this figure is available for free download at www.tcpress.com

energy is freed to focus on teaching content. Herein lies the magic of word study instruction in secondary classrooms.

DISCUSSION QUESTIONS

1. What are high-frequency words or words parts within your specific content area? Identify some key terms that are important for students to decode and understand but may cause difficulty.

2. How might you incorporate structural analysis into your daily instruction?

3. Do the struggling readers and students with disabilities struggle to read the textbooks or curricular materials in your class? Why? Are these texts written on advanced reading levels? Do they contain many nonphonetic or multisyllabic words? Do the sentences and paragraphs present multiple sophisticated ideas at one time? All of the above?

4. Select a topic, lesson, unit, or chapter within your content area. Identify 8–10 words that would be good candidates for direct teaching. Why did you select these words?

CHAPTER 7

Bringing It All Together

In this book we have discussed several ideas related to word study instruction, including effective instructional principles, assessment, word parts, and strategies, among others. Now it is time to consider how to put all of this information together. What would it look like to incorporate word study instruction in secondary classrooms? How can teachers incorporate word study instruction without detracting from their primary responsibility of teaching content? How can word study instruction be situated in secondary classrooms so it benefits *all* learners? This chapter provides practical tips and examples that can answer these questions.

PLANNING

The first step in implementing word study instruction is to engage in careful planning. It is wise to adopt the Boy Scout motto "Be prepared." Advance planning and careful consideration when selecting texts and words to teach will reduce the likelihood students will be confused or misapply word study knowledge and strategies.

Selecting Vocabulary to Teach

Recall from the last chapter that research has shown that teachers can realistically directly teach only 8–10 new words or word parts per week (Beck et al., 2002; Biemiller, 2005), so selectivity is in order. Consider the following questions when selecting words to teach directly:

1. What words are central to the content?
2. What words are unfamiliar to students?
3. What words have high utility within and across content areas?
4. What words are necessary for students to be able to write about the content?

5. What words could provide bridges to other words? For example in teaching the word ecology students might be able to discern the meaning of words like *ecosystem, ecologist, ecosphere,* and even *economics*.
6. What words do students already know?

The following vignette shows how a science teacher is applying these types of questions.

> Mr. Donovon is teaching a life science class. The current unit is on cells, and Mr. Donovon is determining which words he should teach directly. In previewing a chapter from the textbook, he identifies four words that are worthy of being taught directly: *cells, membrane, cytoplasm,* and *hereditary*. As shown in Figure 7.1, his reasons for selecting these words vary, but in each case he is making deliberate decisions about the words' utility and importance.
>
> He selected the word *cells* because this is a high-frequency word and the focus of the entire chapter. He selected *membrane* because understanding this word is critical to overall comprehension of cellular composition and function. He selected *cytoplasm* because this word presents an opportunity to

Figure 7.1. Selecting Vocabulary for Direct Teaching

Here is an excerpt from Mr. Donovon's life science textbook. Selected words to directly teach are underlined.

Living <u>cells</u> are dynamic and have several things in common. A cell is the smallest unit that is capable of performing life functions. All cells have an outer covering called a cell <u>membrane</u>. Inside every cell is a gelatinlike material called <u>cytoplasm</u>. In the cytoplasm of every cell is <u>hereditary</u> material that controls the life of the cell. (*Glencoe Science Life Science,* 2001, p. 38).

Word	Selection Rationale
cells	High-frequency content word; critical to overall comprehension
membrane	Critical content word necessary for comprehension
cytoplasm	Opportunity to teach Greek combining forms *cyto* and *plasm*
hereditary	Word used within and across content areas

teach the Greek combining forms *cyto* and *plasm*, which could aid students in understanding future words like *cytosome* and *endoplasm*. Finally, he selected *hereditary* because it is a term that is used in other content area classes and more advanced science classes.

Evaluating Texts

It is also important to preview texts you will ask students to read. As discussed in Chapter 4, determining whether a text is too advanced for students may explain potential difficulties or frustration. Additionally, it is beneficial to be on the lookout for exception words. *Exception words* are those that are nonphonetic (e.g., *said, was*), have a false morpheme (*ex* in *extra*), or do not follow standard phoneme-grapheme correspondences. By identifying such words ahead of time, teachers can alert students to the exceptions before they make mistakes.

INSTRUCTION

Once you have selected the words or word parts to teach, it is important to teach them directly to students, provide multiple opportunities for practice, and assess whether students have learned and can apply them (discussed in Chapter 4).

Explicit Teaching

If students need to know the word *transform*, rather than telling them it means "to change in form or appearance," capitalize on the opportunity to directly teach the Latin roots using the My Turn–Together–Your Turn format.

> *(Teacher writes* transform *on board.)*

> **Teacher:** This word is *transform* and we are going to break it apart to figure out what it means. *Transform* has two word parts.

> *(Teacher draws a line between* trans *and* form *on board.)*

> **Teacher:** *Trans* is a prefix and it means change. *Form* means to make into a certain shape.
> **Teacher:** So if we put these meanings together, we have 'to change shape or form.'
> **Teacher:** Let's try it all together. What does *transform* mean?

         Students: To change shape or form.
         Teacher: Great job! Yes. *Transform* means to change shape or form.

Opportunities for Practice

Once you have taught the target word or word parts directly, it is time for students to practice, practice, practice. It would be helpful for students to read the word in connected text so they have immediate opportunities to practice reading the word and thinking about its meaning in relation to the specific content in which it is used. For example, in a science lesson on plate tectonics students could read the following:

> Plate tectonics explains how movement within the earth can cause the earth's crust to transform. Earthquakes, volcanoes, and mountain ranges are examples of transformations that can occur.

Students should also be given opportunities to relate the target word to other words and word parts. In the sample text above, students could think about how *transform* and *transformations* are related. Think back to the graphic and semantic organizers presented in Chapter 6. These are excellent tools to promote practice and application. If we continue with the example *transform*, students could complete a graphic organizer as in Figure 7.2 (provided they have already learned all of the other word parts).

Challenge students to write as many words as possible (*deform, reform, formation,* and so on). To reinforce the meanings of word parts, they should also try to determine the meanings of the words they generate. For example, they could explain the difference between *form, formed,* and *formation.* Or, they could talk about the similarities and differences between *transform* and *reform.*

Learning games provide another possibility for practice that students find engaging. I recommend using games as a way to provide ongoing practice after students have demonstrated they have learned the key content and can apply it independently. Here is a list of games to promote practice:

- **Concentration.** Word parts and their meanings are printed on cards. Students shuffle the cards and place them face down. Students take turns flipping over two cards and determining whether they have a match. Example: Cards with *graph* and *written* match. Cards with *scope* and *written* do not match.

Figure 7.2. Graphic Organizer for Practice (Based on *Transform*)

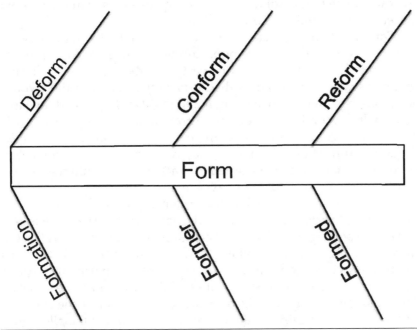

Note: A blank reproducible version of this figure is available for free download at www.tcpress.com

- **Bingo.** The classic call-out game can be modified so students place a token on word parts and call out Bingo when they have five tokens in a row vertically, horizontally, or diagonally.
- **Snatch It.** Word part cards are placed face up in groups of 5 to 7. The teacher calls out the meaning of a word part and students have to race to be the first one to snatch the card.

Word Study Bingo is a twist on the classic game. When I use this game, I write a bank of word parts on the board (e.g., *bio, phys, ology*). Students are given blank Bingo sheets and they select which word parts to record on their sheet and where to place them. In this way students also have the opportunity to spell the word parts. Then I call out the meanings of various word parts. For example, I might say, "This word part means *life*." Students can place a chip or token on *bio* if they wrote it on their sheet. As in the original game, the first person to fill five squares in a row wins. To take the practice opportunity one step further, I ask students to write an example word underneath each word part they select, as shown in Figure 7.3. Then I ask the winner to read aloud his or her words and their meanings.

If you do not have time to play a full game of Word Study Bingo, you can reduce the size of the board to 3 squares x 3 squares to shorten the length of a game, as shown in Figure 7.3.

Concentration is another example of a game that you can modify to create word study practice opportunities. In one version, students must find matches between word parts and their meanings. For example, if students turned over the cards with *jur* and *law,* they would have a match. If they turned over *jur* and *to shape,* they would not have a match. In a second version of Concentration, students turn over cards with various word parts and attempt to make real words. For example, if students turned over *jur* and *or,* they could make the word *juror.* If, on the other hand, they overturned *jur* and *ject,* they could not make a word, and therefore would not have a match.

Finally, the game Snatch It helps students increase their automaticity with word parts and reading multisyllabic words. The game is best played in a small group. A series of cards are placed face up so all cards are visible. The teacher or other person identified as the caller says the meanings of word parts and students race to "snatch" the correct cards. For example, a teacher might say, "This word part means *end.*" Then students quickly scan the overturned cards to locate the one with *fin* printed on it. The first student to see it takes it out of the pile before other students have the chance. Another version is to call out multisyllabic words so students can practice their decoding skills. To be sure students do not simply look for words that begin with the first letter of the word you called out, I recommend having groups of cards with words that all begin with the same letter. This will ensure that students actually read the middle and ending of the words. Figure 7.4 illustrates a sample game of Snatch It used in an economics class.

Because Snatch It is based on students' speed in applying skills, I recommend grouping students by ability level when they play this game. It would be unfair and very punishing if struggling readers and students with disabilities were trying to race against the best readers in a class. Finally, here is a quick tip: For Concentration and Snatch It, standard size index cards work as the perfect size game card. No need to spend time cutting up pieces of paper!

Flexible Grouping Arrangements

The degree to which teachers are able to effectively include word study instruction in their classroom will depend largely on the grouping arrangements they use. Supporting the word study needs of the struggling readers and students with disabilities is more difficult if

Figure 7.3. Bingo Sheet with Word Parts and Example Words

Bio	Eco	Proto
biome	ecology	protoza
Sphere		Cycle
	FREE	
hemisphere		recycle
Derm	Geo	Ecto
dermatol-ogy	geology	Ectopic

Note: A blank reproducible version of this figure is available for free download at www. tcpress.com

Figure 7.4. Snatch It Cards for Economics

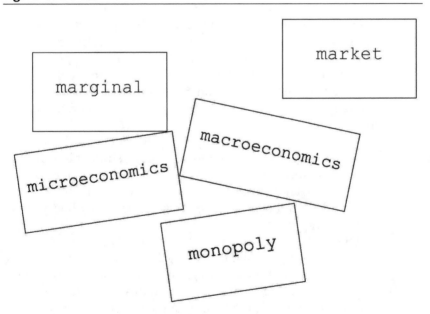

the only instructional arrangement teachers use is teacher-directed, whole-group instruction. Alternatively, when teachers use flexible instructional arrangements that regularly incorporate small-group instruction, their success incorporating word study instruction tends to be much higher.

As mentioned in Chapter 4, there are several benefits of using small-group instruction, including greater opportunities for immediate feedback and error correction, mini lessons on skills or content that particular groups of students need, and the opportunity for students to learn from one another. There are a variety of grouping arrangements that can facilitate teachers' implementation of word study instruction in the classroom. Here are a few possibilities:

1. Teacher works one-on-one with a student while the rest of the class completes independent seatwork. Having time to work one-on-one with a student is a useful arrangement for conducting assessments, providing targeted skill instruction, or listening to a student read aloud.

2. Teacher works one-on-one with a student while the rest of the class works in small groups. Small groups are particularly useful when having students play games for extra practice opportunities, take part in cooperative learning activities, and work on group projects.

3. Teacher works with a small group while the rest of the class completes independent seatwork. Teacher-guided small groups are useful arrangements when several students all need the same skill instruction, intervention, or opportunities to practice with the teacher who can provide immediate feedback and error correction. Small groups are also an ideal format for implementing the My Turn–Together–Your Turn procedure.

4. Teacher works with a small group while another adult (e.g., teaching assistant, paraprofessional, student intern, volunteer) supervises the rest of the class either in whole group or in small groups. This arrangement can also be reversed, with the teacher supervising the class while another adult works with a small group.

5. Teacher works one-on-one with a student or guides small-group instruction while the rest of the class works in pairs. This arrangement provides a great opportunity for students to practice reading aloud to a peer. In this case, I recommend pairing a struggling reader or student with disability with a stronger reader who can provide modeling and error correction.

6. All students work in small groups and rotate among stations with different activities. One station is teacher-guided small-group instruction. If there are additional adults in the room,

each could guide a lesson or activity at a station. Notice that I did not refer to students rotating among "centers." I have found the term *center* has an elementary connotation, and students, therefore, do not take the work as seriously.

Some teachers shy away from small-group work because the logistics of managing multiple student groups feels daunting. When implementing an instructional arrangement that incorporates small-group work, you should consider investing time up front to explicitly teach students the expectations for working with their peers in small groups. This includes teaching students how to talk at an appropriate volume, locate and return materials, be equal contributors, resolve conflict, and request assistance from the teacher or other adult. Then, provide some time for students to practice the skills and behaviors you are expecting. You could even incorporate some classwide motivational systems (see Chapter 4). For example, you could award points to small groups that follow the expectations. Upon reaching a specified number of points, students in the small group earn a reward. Having clear roles for students within groups can also be a helpful strategy to reduce conflict. One student can be the recorder who writes down information. Another student could be the reader who reads material for the group. Another student could be the illustrator who draws for the group. Other potential roles include timekeeper, materials manager, questioner, and summarizer. You can also create roles that are content-specific. For example, if students are creating a landform map using clay, perhaps each student could be assigned one landform to create. Then all group members work together to assemble the parts into one large map. Matching students to their strengths makes the assigning roles strategy particularly powerful. Asking your lowest reader to be the "reader" for the group is likely to lead to frustration for all.

It is easy to assume that students will know how to work cooperatively, but this is rarely the case. Even more importantly, students will not know how *you* expect them to work together. By taking the time to teach and practice the skills and behaviors necessary for successful small-group work in your classroom, you will reap the benefits of having an engaging instructional format ready for use at any time

TIPS AND TRICKS

While explicit word study instruction is important in promoting the achievement of struggling readers and students with disabilities, there are also many possibilities to reinforce word study skills and strategies in more informal ways throughout the day. Here are some tips and tricks:

1. Encourage students to be word detectives. When they encounter a target word or word part in print outside of class, allow them to bring it to class and share.
2. Have students maintain a word logbook or notebook. As students learn new words and word parts, they can record them in their book.
3. Tape high-frequency word parts and their meanings in students' planners, lab books, or binders for a quick reference.
4. Display a word wall in your classroom with word part families.
5. Have students keep a piece of scratch paper and pencil near them when they read. When they encounter a word they cannot decode, they can write it down and break it apart using the "syllable types" or "identify known parts" strategies.
6. Post the word division patterns in your classroom for reference.
7. When writing multisyllabic words on the board, go ahead and mark the consonants and vowels to assist students in decoding them.
8. Analyze students' writing to identify potential gaps in word study knowledge. For example, if a student writes: "Plants have a sell wall," it might be a good time to do a minilesson on the word *cell* and the letter *c* taking the soft sound when it is followed by *e, i,* or *y.*
9. Have students go on a scavenger hunt in which they have to find and write down places or items that contain word parts. For example, students could hunt for items with *tri, scope,* and *photo* in their names and find a triangle, microscope, and photograph.
10. Give students a word part and ask them to brainstorm words with that part. For the prefix *tri-,* students could list *tricycle, triangle, trilogy, triceratops.* Warning: be on the look out for exception words. Words like *tried, tribe,* and *trip* begin with *tri,* but it is not functioning as a prefix.
11. Prior to having students read a text about an unfamiliar topic, show a brief video clip that includes the key vocabulary. Not only will you help activate any related background

knowledge students may have, but also you will provide opportunities for students to hear the multisyllabic words they will encounter in the text. Decoding these words later in the text may be easier for some students since they will have heard the words before.

12. Try not to reference instruction in decoding or word study as "phonics." Older students often associate this term with elementary reading instruction and may feel embarrassed or become resistant to word study instruction if they believe it is designed for younger students.

Word study instruction need not command a sizeable portion of class time to make a lasting difference in students' decoding, spelling, and vocabulary knowledge. Through a combination of explicit teaching procedures and informal learning opportunities embedded throughout the day, students will acquire word study skills that increase their access to general education content area texts.

DISCUSSION QUESTIONS

1. What challenges do you foresee in trying to embed word study instruction in your classroom? What are some potential solutions?

2. This chapter presented the idea of making students word detectives. Brainstorm other activities or initiatives that might get students excited about words and word study.

3. Select a lesson that you plan to teach in the future. Identify two or three places where you could embed word study instruction in that lesson.

Conclusion

Mrs. Taylor teaches middle school geography and world cultures. Currently her students are learning about location as one of the five themes of geography. In today's lesson students are using a series of tools including globes and maps to explore ideas related to absolute location. Mrs. Taylor has divided the class into small groups with four students in each group, and each student has been given a role as locator, recorder, reader, or materials manager. Prior to breaking off into their groups, Mrs. Taylor quickly reviews the expectations for working in small groups including the need to work quietly, respectfully, and collaboratively—values she has taught and modeled since the first day of school. She also reminds students that the point goal for today's lesson is 10, meaning any group that earns 10 points for following expectations and completing the assignment may choose from an extensive menu of rewards including things like 5 minutes of free time on early release days, small school supplies like pencils or folders, a soda for lunch time, or the opportunity to sit next to a friend during one class period.

The assignment students must complete in their small groups is a scavenger hunt to find specific places on a globe or map using latitude and longitude coordinates. Prior to today's lesson, Mrs. Taylor directly taught the following key terms: *absolute location, latitude, longitude, coordinates*, and *degrees*. Today's small-group assignment is an opportunity for students to practice applying their newly learned vocabulary knowledge.

As students work in their small groups, Mrs. Taylor calls Timothy to a kidney-shaped desk in the back of the room. Timothy is a student with a reading disability, and Mrs. Taylor wants to verify that Timothy can successfully decode the lesson's key vocabulary terms when he encounters them in the textbook. She conducts a brief running record (as presented in Chapter 4) with Timothy in which she has him read aloud a textbook passage that contains the target vocabulary. He de-codes everything correctly except for the word *longitude*. He decodes this word as long/it/ude. Mrs. Taylor praises Timo-thy for putting forth such great effort in reading and then im-mediately has him re-examine the word *longitude*. She reminds him that the letter *g* takes the soft *g* sound when it comes be-fore the letters *e, i,* or *y*. She asks him to decode the word *longi-tude* again, and this time he is able to do so correctly. She gives him a high-five and sends him back to work in his small group.

Once Timothy has returned to his small group, Mrs. Taylor scans the room and awards four of the small groups two points for being on task and following expectations. Then she circu-lates around the room, visiting briefly with each small group to check on students' progress and answer questions. She returns to the kidney-shaped table in the back of the room and calls Elise, an ELL student, to join her. As she did with Timothy, Mrs. Taylor conducts a running record and evaluates Elise's reading accuracy.

Mrs. Taylor represents a veteran teacher who has found ways to seam-lessly incorporate word study instruction into her content area class. She expertly uses small-group instruction, setting students up for suc-cess by stating clear expectations and assigning students clear roles. Her classroom provides positive reinforcement for being engaged, re-spectful, and collaborative learners. Her use of small-group instruction enables Mrs. Taylor to spend one-on-one time with specific students whose progress needs to be closely monitored. Mrs. Taylor still consid-ers her primary responsibility to be teaching social studies content, but by incorporating many of the strategies presented in this book, she has found ways to support students' reading needs as well.

I spend a lot of time in secondary schools and classrooms, and I am always in awe of how hard teachers work and how many respon-sibilities are placed on them. Asking secondary teachers to implement word study instruction when they already feel immense pressure to cover vast amounts of content and meet heightened academic stan-dards may seem unrealistic or perhaps untenable. I believe, however, with basic knowledge and a few effective strategies and instructional arrangements like the ones Mrs. Taylor used, teachers can promote the success of struggling readers and students with disabilities in second-ary classrooms.

Word study instruction is a way to unlock the power of words and reading for students who are often marginalized within school communities due to their reading difficulties. With greater success will come more motivation, participation, practice, and ensuing improvement. Thus teachers will set the Matthew Effect in motion in a positive way. Although the strategies presented in this book are specifically aimed at struggling readers and students with disabilities, teachers may find they benefit all students.

Encouraging secondary teachers to support the reading needs of struggling readers and students with disabilities does not mean these students will no longer need intensive, individualized, evidence-based interventions in targeted areas of need. The reality is that these students will need intervention and support from multiple individuals over the course of the entire school day (O'Connor, 2007). In this way, content area teachers' task is a little easier. Multiple school personnel collaborating to support individual students means the responsibility for student progress is shared. More shared support will lead to better student outcomes in less time. My goal in writing this book is simply to empower all teachers with knowledge and skills that can help them be active participants in supporting all students included in general education classrooms. For me, that is a necessary step in promoting educational equity for all of our nation's students.

Additional Resources

Resources for Phonemic Awareness

Belvins, W. (1997). *Phonemic awareness activities for early reading success: Easy playful activities that prepare children for phonics instruction.* New York, NY: Scholastic.

Gunning, T. G. (2000). *Phonological awareness and primary phonics.* Boston, MA: Allyn & Bacon.

Resources for Phonics and Word Study

Cunningham, P. M. (2005). *Phonics they use: Words for reading and writing.* New York, NY: Pearson.

Eldredge, J. L. (1999). *Phonics for teachers: Self-instruction, methods, and activities.* Upper Saddle River, NJ: Merrill.

Fox, B. J. (2010). *Phonics and structural analysis for the teacher of reading: Programmed for self-instruction.* Boston, MA: Allyn & Bacon.

Henry, M. K. (2003). *Unlocking literacy: Effective decoding & spelling instruction.* Baltimore, MD: Paul H. Brookes.

Honig, B., Diamond, L., & Gutlohn, L. (2000). *Teaching reading: Sourcebook for kindergarten through eighth grade.* Novato, CA: Arena Press.

Johnson, K., & Bayrd, P. (1986). *Megawords: Multisyllabic words for reading, spelling, and vocabulary.* Cambridge, MA: Educators Publishing Service.

O'Connor, R. E. (2007). *Teaching word recognition: Effective strategies for students with learning difficulties.* New York, NY: Guilford Press.

Rudginsky, L. T., & Haskell, E. C. (2002). *How to teach spelling.* Cambridge, MA: Educators Publishing Service.

Resources for Fluency

Altwerger, B., Jordan, N., & Shelton, N. R. (2007). *Rereading fluency: Process, practice, and policy.* Portsmouth, NH: Heinemann.

Kuhn, M. R., & Schwaneflugel, P. J. (2008). *Fluency in the classroom.* New York, NY: Guilford Press.

Rasinski, T. V. (2003). *The fluent reader*. New York, NY: Scholastic.

Rasinski, T. V., & Padak, N. D. (2001). *From phonics to fluency: Effective teaching of decoding and reading fluency in the elementary school*. New York, NY: Longman.

Riggenbach, H. (2000). *Perspective on fluency*. Ann Arbor, MI: University of Michigan Press.

Resources for Vocabulary

Allen, J. (1999). *Words, words, words*. Portsmouth, NH: Heinemann.

Blachowicz, C., & Fisher, P. J. (2002). *Teaching vocabulary in all classrooms*. Upper Saddle River, NJ: Merrill Prentice Hall.

Buis, K. (2004). *Making words stick: Strategies that build vocabulary and reading comprehension in the elementary grades*. Portland, ME: Pembroke.

Fry, E. B. (2004). *The vocabulary teacher's book of lists*. San Francisco, CA: Jossey-Bass.

Stahl, S., & Kapinus, B. (2001). *Word power: What every educator needs to know about teaching vocabulary*. Washington, DC: NEA Professional Libraries.

Resources for Comprehension

Blachowicz, C., & Ogle, D. (2001). *Reading comprehension: Strategies for independent learners*. New York, NY: Guilford Press.

Block, C. C., & Pressley, M. (2002). *Comprehension instruction: Research-based best practices*. New York, NY: Guilford Press.

Harvey, S., & Goudvis, A. (2000). *Strategies that work: Teaching comprehension to enhance understanding*. York, ME: Stenhouse.

Moss, J. F. (2005). *Literature, literacy, and comprehension strategies in the elementary school*. Urbana, IL: National Council of Teachers of English.

Resources for Students with Reading Difficulties and Disabilities

Bursuck, W. D., & Damer, M. (2011). *Teaching reading to students who are at risk or have disabilities*. Upper Saddle River, NJ: Pearson.

Hougen, M. (2015). *Fundamentals of literacy instruction and assessment, 6–12*. Baltimore, MD: Paul H. Brookes.

Hougen, M., & Smartt, S. (2012). *Fundamentals of literacy instruction and assessment, pre-K–6*. Baltimore, MD: Paul H. Brookes.

Linan-Thompson, S., & Vaughn, S. (2007). *Research-based methods of reading instruction for English language learners, Grades K–4*. Alexandria, VA: ASCD.

Vaughn, S., & Linan-Thompson, S. (2004). *Research-based methods of reading instruction, grades K–3*. Alexandria, VA: ASCD.

Resources for Reading Assessment

Afflerbach, P. (2012). *Understanding and using reading assessment, K–12* (2nd ed.). Newark, DE: International Reading Association.

Diamond, L., & Thorsnes, B. J. (2008). *Assessing reading: Multiple measures for kindergarten through twelfth grade.* Berkeley, CA: Consortium on Reading Excellence.

Dougherty Stahl, K. A., & Bravo, M. A. (2010). Contemporary classroom vocabulary assessment for content areas. *The Reading Teacher, 63,* 566–578.

Table A.1. Websites Related to Reading Instruction and Research

Website	URL	Description
Big Ideas in Beginning Reading	reading. uoregon.edu	Provides definitions and descriptions of research and practice around the five areas of reading
Florida Center for Reading Research (FCRR)	fcrr.org	Presents multidisciplinary research, effective practices, and resources in reading for teachers, parents, and students
International Literacy Association	literacyworld-wide.org	Worldwide association dedicated to researching and sharing literacy practices
Reading Rockets	readingrockets. org	Provides information and resources about how children learn to read and how to support students who struggle with reading
Vaughn Gross Center for Reading and Language Arts	meadowscenter. org/vgc/	Promotes effective reading and language arts instruction through the sharing of research, instructional resources, and technical assistance

References

Adams, M. J. (1990). *Beginning to read*. Cambridge, MA: MIT Press.

Al Otaiba, S., Connor, C. M., Folsom, J. S., Greulich, L., Meadows, J., & Li, Z. (2011). Assessment data-informed guidance to individualize kindergarten reading instruction: Findings from a cluster-randomized control field trial. *The Elementary School Journal*, 111(4), 535.

Alvermann, D. E., Phelps, S. F., & Ridgeway, V. G. (2007). *Content area reading and literacy: Succeeding in today's diverse classrooms*. Upper Saddle River, NJ: Pearson.

Armbruster, B. B., Lehr, F., Osborn, J., O'Rourke, R., Beck, I., Carnine, D., & Simmons, D. (2003). *Put reading first*. Ann Arbor, MI: Center for the Improvement of Early Reading Achievement.

Barton, M. L., Heidema, C., & Jordan, D. (2002). Teaching reading in mathematics and science. *Educational Leadership*, 60(3), 24–28.

Beck, I., McKeown, M. G., & Kucan, L. (2002). *Bringing words to life: Robust vocabulary development*. New York, NY: Guilford Press.

Biancarosa, G., & Snow, C. E. (2006). *Reading next: A vision for action and research in middle and high school literacy: A report to Carnegie Corporation of New York* (2nd ed.). Washington, DC: Alliance for Excellent Education.

Biemiller, A. (2005). Vocabulary development and instruction: A prerequisite for school learning. In S. B. Neuman & D. K. Dickinson (Eds.), *The handbook of early literacy research* (Vol. 2) (pp. 41–51). New York, NY: Guilford Press.

Boardman, A. G., Roberts, G., Vaughn, S., Wexler, J., Murray, C. S., & Kosanovich, M. (2008). *Effective instruction for adolescent struggling readers: A practice brief*. Portsmouth, NH: RMC Research Corporation, Center on Instruction.

Burns, M. S., Griffin, P., & Snow, C. E. (1999). *Starting out right: A guide to promoting children's reading success*. Washington, DC: National Academies Press.

Bursuck, W. D., & Damer, M. (2011). *Teaching reading to students who are at risk or have disabilities*. Upper Saddle River, NJ: Pearson.

Cain, K., & Oakhill, J. (2011). Matthew effects in young readers: Reading comprehension and reading experience aid vocabulary development. *Journal of Learning Disabilities*, 44, 431–443.

Chall, J. S., Jacobs, V. A., & Baldwin, L. E. (1990). *The reading crisis: Why poor children fall behind.* Cambridge, MA: Harvard University Press.

Chard, D. J., Vaughn, S., & Tyler, B. J. (2002). A synthesis of research on effective interventions for building reading fluency with elementary students with learning disabilities. *Journal of Learning Disabilities, 35*(5), 386–406.

Cirino, P., Fuchs, L. S., Tolar, T., & Powell, S. R. (2011, April). *Profile analysis of children with MD with and without RD on mathematical competencies in 2nd and 3rd grade.* Paper presented at the annual meeting of the Society for Research in Child Development, Montreal, Quebec, Canada.

Common Core State Standards Initiative. (n.d.). *Common core state standards.* Available at www.corestandards.org

Connor, C., Alberto, P. A., Compton, D. L., & O'Connor, R. E. (2014). *Improving reading outcomes for students with or at risk for reading disabilities: A synthesis of the contributions from the Institute of Education Sciences Research Centers.* Washington, DC: U.S. Department of Education, Institute of Education Sciences, National Center for Special Education Research.

Cunningham, V. (1998). Reading now and then. In B. Cox (Ed.). *Literacy is not enough: Essays on the importance of reading* (pp. 9–19). Manchester, UK: Manchester University Press.

DeFrancis, J. (1984). *The Chinese language: Fact and fantasy.* Honolulu, HI: University of Hawaii Press.

Delquadri, J. C., Greenwood, C. R., Stretton, K., & Hall, R. V. (1983). The peer tutoring spelling game: A classroom procedure for increasing opportunity to respond and spelling performance. *Education and Treatment of Children, 6*(3), 225–239.

Deno, S. L., Fuchs, L. S., Marston, D., & Shin, J. (2001). Using curriculum-based measurement to establish growth standards for students with learning disabilities. *School Psychology Review, 30,* 507–526.

Deshler, D. D., & Hock, M. F. (2007). *Adolescent literacy: Where we are, where we need to go.* Available at www.ldonline.org/article/12288/

Diamond, L., & Gutlohn, L. (2006). *Vocabulary handbook.* Baltimore, MD: Paul H. Brookes.

Discover Boating, (2015). *Learning the basics of sailing.* Available at www.discoverboating.com/resources/article.aspx?id=259

Duke, N. K., Pressley, M., & Hilden, K. (2004). Difficulties with reading comprehension. In C. A. Stone, E. R. Silliman, K. Apel, & B. J. Ehren (Eds.), *Handbook of language and literacy: development and disorders* (pp. 501–520). New York, NY: Guilford Press.

Earth materials and processes. (2002). New York, NY: McGraw-Hill.

Ehri, L. C., & Snowling, M. J. (2004). Developmental variation in word recognition. In C. A. Stone, E. R. Silliman, K. Apel, & B. J. Ehren (Eds.), *Handbook of language and literacy: Development and disorders* (pp. 433–460). New York, NY: Guilford Press.

Elbaum, B., Vaughn, S., Hughes, M., Moody, S. W., & Schumm, J. S. (2000). How reading outcomes of students with disabilities are related to instructional grouping formats: A meta-analytic review. In R. Gersten, E. Schiller, & S. Vaughn (Eds.), *Contemporary special education research* (pp. 105–135). Mahwah, NJ: Erlbaum.

Engelmann, S. (1999). The benefits of direct instruction: Affirmative action for at-risk students. *Educational Leadership, 57*, 77–79.

Faggella-Luby, M. N., Ware, S. M., & Capozzoli, A. (2009). Adolescent literacy—Reviewing adolescent literacy reports: Key components and critical questions. *Journal of Literacy Research, 41*, 453–475.

Foorman, B. R., & Torgesen, J. (2001). Critical elements of classroom and small-group instruction promote reading success in all children. *Learning Disabilities Research & Practice, 16*(4), 203–212.

Fuchs, D., Fuchs, L. S., Mathes, P. G., & Simmons, D. C. (1997). Peer-assisted learning strategies: Making classrooms more responsive to diversity. *American Educational Research Journal, 34*, 174–206.

Garner, R. (1987). *Metacognition and reading comprehension.* New York, NY: Ablex.

Glencoe science life science. (2001). New York, NY: McGraw-Hill.

Goodlad, J. I. (2004). *A place called school: Prospects for the future* (20th Anniversary Ed.). New York, NY: McGraw-Hill.

Greenleaf, C., Schoenbach, R., Cziko, C., & Mueller, F. (2001). Apprenticing adolescent readers to academic literacy. *Harvard Educational Review, 71*(1), 79–130.

Gregory, A., Skiba, R. J., & Noguera, P. A. (2010). The achievement gap and the discipline gap: Two sides of the same coin? *Educational Researcher, 39*(1), 59–68.

Hamilton, L., Halverson, R., Jackson, S., Mandinach, E., Supovitz, J., & Wayman, J. (2009). *Using student achievement data to support instructional decision making* (NCEE 2009-4067). Washington, DC: National Center for Education Evaluation and Regional Assistance, Institute of Education Sciences, U.S. Department of Education.

Hart, B., & Risley, T. R. (1995). *Meaningful differences in the everyday experience of young American children.* Baltimore, MD: Paul H. Brookes Publishing.

Hart, B., & Risley, T. R. (2003). The early catastrophe: The 30 million word gap by age 3. *American Educator, 27*, 4–9.

Heller, R. (2015). *Vocabulary.* Washington, DC: WETA. Available at www.adlit.org/adlit_101/improving_literacy_instruction_in_your_school/vocabulary/

Henry, M. K. (2003). *Unlocking literacy: Effective decoding & spelling instruction.* Baltimore, MD: Paul H. Brookes.

Hiebert, E. H., & Mesmer, H.A.E. (2013). Upping the ante of text complexity in the Common Core State Standards: Examining its potential impact on young readers. *Educational Researcher, 42*(1), 44–51.

Hirsch, E. D. (2005). Reading comprehension requires knowledge—of words and the world: Scientific insights into the fourth-grade slump and the nation's stagnant comprehension scores. In Z. Fang (Ed.), *Literacy teaching and learning: Current issues and trends* (pp. 121–130). Upper Saddle River, NJ: Pearson.

Honig, B., Diamond, L., & Gutlohn, L. (2000). *Teaching reading: Sourcebook for kindergarten through eighth grade.* Novato, CA: Arena Press.

IDEA. (2004). *Individuals with Disabilities Education Improvement Act of 2004*, 20 U.S.C. § 614 et seq.

Jenkins, J., Hudson, R., & Lee, S. (2007). Using CBM-reading assessments to monitor progress. *Perspectives on Language and Literacy, 33*(2), 11–18.

Kamhi, A. G., & Catts, H. W. (2012). *Language and reading disabilities* (3rd ed.). Upper Saddle River, NJ: Pearson.

Kamil, M. L. (2003). *Adolescents and literacy: Reading for the 21st century.* Washington, DC: Alliance for Excellent Education.

Kamil, M. L., Borman, G. D., Dole, J., Kral, C. C., Salinger, T., & Torgesen, J. (2008). *Improving adolescent literacy: Effective classroom and intervention practices* (NCEE 2008-4027). Washington, DC: National Center for Education Evaluation and Regional Assistance, Institute of Education Sciences, U.S. Department of Education.

Kenney, J. M., Hancewicz, E., Heuer, L., Metsisto, D., & Tuttle, C. L. (2005). *Literacy strategies for improving mathematics instruction.* Alexandria, VA: ASCD.

Klingner, J. K., Artiles, A. J., & Barletta, L. M. (2006). English language learners who struggle with reading language acquisition or LD? *Journal of Learning Disabilities, 39*, 108–128.

Klingner, J. K., & Vaughn, S. (1996). Reciprocal teaching of reading comprehension strategies for students with learning disabilities who use English as a second language. *Elementary School Journal, 96*, 275–293.

Lane, H. B., Pullen, P. C., Eisele, M. R., & Jordan, L. (2005). Preventing reading failure: Phonological awareness assessment and instruction. In Z. Fang (Ed.), *Literacy teaching and learning: Current issues and trends* (pp. 69–80). Upper Saddle River, NJ: Pearson.

Lane, K. L., Wehby, J., Menzies, H. M., Doukas, G. L., Munton, S. M., & Gregg, R. M. (2003). Social skills instruction for students at risk for antisocial behavior: The effects of small-group instruction. *Behavioral Disorders, 3*, 229–248.

Leko, M. M., Mundy, C. A., & Kiely, M. T. (2009). Reading disabilities: Research, recommendations and resources for teachers. *The Florida Reading Journal, 45*(2), 6–14.

Lenz, B. K., & Hughes, C. A. (1990). A word identification strategy for adolescents with learning disabilities. *Journal of Learning Disabilities, 23*, 149–158.

Lenz, B. K., Schumaker, J. B., Deshler, D. D., & Beals, V. L. (1984). *Learning strategies curriculum: The word-identification strategy.* Lawrence: University of Kansas.

Linan-Thompson, S., & Vaughn, S. (2007). *Research-based methods of reading instruction for English language learners, grades K–4.* Alexandria, VA: ASCD.

Lou, Y., Abrami, P. C., Spence, J. C., Poulsen, C., Chambers, B., & d'Apollonia, S. (1996). Within-class grouping: A meta-analysis. *Review of Educational Research, 66*(4), 423–458.

Lyon, G. R. (2000). *Why reading is not a natural process.* Pittsburgh, PA: Learning Disabilities Association of America.

Lyon, G. R. (2003). Reading disabilities: Why do some children have difficulty learning to read? What can be done about it? *Perspectives on Language and Literacy, 29*(2), 17–19.

Maheady, L., & Gard, J. (2010). Classwide peer tutoring: Practice, theory, research, and personal narrative. *Intervention in School and Clinic, 46*(2), 71–78.

Mercer, C. D., & Pullen, P. C. (2005). *Students with learning disabilities* (6th ed.). Upper Saddle River, NJ: Pearson.

Moats, L. C. (2005). How spelling supports reading: And why it is more regular and predictable than you may think. *American Educator, 29*(4), 12–22, 42–43.

Montgomery, D. J., Karlan, G. R., & Coutinho, M. (2001). The effectiveness of word processor spell checker programs to produce target words for misspellings generated by students with learning disabilities. *Journal of Special Education Technology, 16,* 27–41.

Nagy, W. E., & Anderson, R. C. (1984). How many words are there in printed school English? *Reading Research Quarterly, 19,* 304–330.

Nagy, W. E., Winsor, P., Osborn, J., & O'Flahavan, J. (1994). Structural analysis: Some guidelines for instruction. In F. Lehr & J. Osborn (Eds.), *Reading, language, and literacy* (pp. 45–58). Hillsdale, NJ: Erlbaum.

National Reading Panel (NRP). (2000). *Report of the national reading panel: Teaching children to read: An evidence-based assessment of the scientific research literature on reading and its implications for reading instruction.* Washington, DC: National Institute of Child Health and Human Development.

Newman, L. (2006). *Facts from NLTS2: General education participation and academic performance of students with learning disabilities.* Menlo Park, CA: SRI International.

O'Connor, R. E. (2007). *Teaching word recognition: Effective strategies for students with learning difficulties.* New York, NY: Guilford Press.

O'Connor, R. E., & Bell, K. M. (2004). Teaching students with reading disability to read words. In C.A. Stone, E. R. Silliman, K. Apel, & B. J. Ehren (Eds.), *Handbook of language and literacy: Development and disorders* (pp. 481–500). New York, NY: Guilford Press.

Palincsar, A. S. (2012). Reciprocal teaching. In J. Hattie & E. M. Anderman (Eds.), *International guide to student achievement* (pp. 369–371). New York, NY: Routledge.

Palincsar, A. S., & Brown, A. (1984). Reciprocal teaching of comprehension-fostering and comprehension-monitoring activities. *Cognition and Instruction, 1*(2), 117–175.

Paris, S. G., & Oka, E. R. (1986). Children's reading strategies, metacognition, and motivation. *Developmental Review, 6*(1), 25–56.

Rafdal, B. H., McMaster, K. L., McConnell, S. R., Fuchs, D., & Fuchs, L. S. (2011). The effectiveness of kindergarten peer-assisted learning strategies for students with disabilities. *Exceptional Children, 77*(3), 299–316.

Rasinski, T. (2004). Creating fluent readers. *Educational Leadership, 61*, 46–51.

Reeves, J. R. (2006). Secondary teacher attitudes toward including English-language learners in mainstream classrooms. *The Journal of Educational Research, 99*(3), 131–143.

Rhodes, L. K., & Shanklin, N. L. (1993). *Windows into literacy: Assessing learners, K–8.* Portsmouth, NH: Heinemann.

Scammacca, N., Roberts, G., Vaughn. S., Edmonds, M., Wexler, J., Reutebuch, C. K., & Torgesen, J. K. (2007). *Interventions for adolescent struggling readers: A meta-analysis with implications for practice.* Portsmouth, NH: RMC Research Corporation, Center on Instruction.

Simonsen, F., & Gunter, L. (2001). Best practices in spelling instruction: A research summary. *Journal of Direct Instruction, 1*, 97–105.

Slavin, R. E., Lake, C., & Groff, C. (2009). Effective programs in middle and high school mathematics: A best-evidence synthesis. *Review of Educational Research, 79*, 839–911.

Stahl, S., & Kapinus, B. (2001). *Word power: What every educator needs to know about teaching vocabulary.* Washington, DC: NEA Professional Libraries.

Stanovich, K. E. (1986). Matthew effects in reading: Some consequences of individual differences in the acquisition of literacy. *Reading Research Quarterly, 22*, 360–407.

Strecker, S. K., Roser, N. L., & Martinez, M. G. (2005). Toward understanding oral reading fluency. In Z. Fang (Ed.), *Literacy teaching and learning: Current issues and trends* (pp. 102–111). Upper Saddle River, NJ: Pearson.

Tyner, B. (2009). *Small-group reading instruction: A differentiated teaching model for beginning and struggling readers.* Newark, DE: International Reading Association.

U.S. Department of Education, Institute of Education Sciences, National Center for Education Statistics (NCES). (2000). *Entering kindergarten: A portrait of American children when they begin school: Findings from the condition of education.* Washington, DC: Author.

U.S. Department of Education, Institute of Education Sciences, National Assessment of Educational Progress (NAEP). (2015). *The nation's report card: Reading: Grade 8 National Results* [Data file]. Available at nationsreportcard. gov/reading_2011/nat_g8.asp?tab_id=tab2&subtab_id=Tab_7#chart

Van den Bergh, L., Denessen, E., Hornstra, L., Voeten, M., & Holland, R. W. (2010). The implicit prejudiced attitudes of teachers: Relations to teacher expectations and the ethnic achievement gap. *American Educational Research Journal, 47*(2), 497–527.

Vaughn, S., Hughes, M., Moody, S., & Elbaum, B. (2001). Instructional grouping for reading for students with LD: Implications for practice. *Intervention in School and Clinic, 36*(3), 131–137.

Vaughn, S., Klingner, J. K., Swanson, E. A., Boardman, A. G., Roberts, G., Mohammed, S. S., & Stillman-Spisak, S. J. (2011). Efficacy of collaborative strategic reading with middle school students. *American Educational Research Journal, 48*(4), 938–964.

Vellutino, F. R., Fletcher, J. M., Snowling, M. J., & Scanlon, D. M. (2004). Specific reading disability (dyslexia): What have we learned in the past four decades? *Journal of Child Psychology and Psychiatry, 45*(1), 2–40.

Wagner, M., & Cameto, R. (2004). The characteristics, experiences, and outcomes of youth with emotional disturbances. *NLTS2 Data Brief: A Report from the National Longitudinal Transition Study-2, 3*(2). Minneapolis: University of Minnesota, Institute on Community Integration, National Center on Secondary Education and Transition (NCSET).

Wanzek, J., Vaughn, S., Wexler, J., Swanson, E. A., Edmonds, M., & Kim, A. H. (2006). A synthesis of spelling and reading interventions and their effects on the spelling outcomes of students with LD. *Journal of Learning Disabilities, 39*, 528–543.

Weil, R. (2015). *What are the benefits of swimming?* Available at www.medicinenet. com/swimming/page4.htm

Yoshimasu, K., Barbaresi, W. J., Colligan, R. C., Killian, J. M., Voigt, R. G., Weaver, A. L., & Katusic, S. K. (2010). Gender, attention-deficit/ hyperactivity disorder, and reading disability in a population-based birth cohort. *Pediatrics, 126*(4), 788–795.

Index

Abrami, P. C., 46
Accommodations, for struggling readers/students with disabilities, 53, 55
Achievement gap, reading proficiency and, 2
Adams, M. J., 9, 25, 27
Adolescents
  reading instruction for, 17–18
  targeted interventions for, 2–3
Advanced word study, 17, 57
Affixes, to words, 34–35. *See also* Prefixes; Suffixes
  combining with Latin roots, 84–85
  mathematics terminology, 80–81, 82
  for meaning, structural analysis and, 87–88
  structural analysis of, 60–61, 62
Al Otaiba, S., 46
Alberto, P. A., 26
"Alphabetic principle," 12
  phonics and, 14
Alvermann, D. E., 27
American English
  continuing evolution of, 36–38
  history of, 29–30
  rules and exceptions in, 30, 38
  word derivations in, 29
Anderson, R. C., 58
Anglo-Saxon origins, for words in American English, 29

irregular words and, 36
Apps, for spelling help, 74
Armbruster, B. B., 12, 15
Artiles, A. J., 2
Assessment
  comprehension questions, 16
  determining students' areas of difficulty, 26–27, 47–48
  of readability of text and curricular material, 48–55
  of reading, resources for, 111
  of reading proficiency, 47–48
  of students' strengths and weaknesses, 26–27, 47–48
  types of, 26
Attention, in reading process, 11
Attention deficit/hyperactivity disorder (ADHD), reading problems and, 20

Background knowledge
  in reading process, 10–11
  text comprehension and, 27
Baldwin, L. E., 58
Barbaresi, W. J., 20
Barletta, L. M., 2
Barton, M. L., 3
Base words
  affixes to, 34–35
  in structural analysis for meaning, 87–88
Basic word study, 17
Beals, V. L., 62

About the Author

Melinda M. Leko is an assistant professor in the department of special education at the University of Kansas (KU). She teaches courses on reading instruction for students with high-incidence disabilities and collaboration in special education courses. Her research centers on teacher preparation to support students with disabilities in inclusive classrooms, reading instruction, and specific learning disabilities. Her work has appeared in several prominent journals including: *Exceptional Children, The Journal of Special Education, Remedial and Special Education,* and *Learning Disability Quarterly.* Prior to joining the faculty at KU, Melinda worked as an assistant professor in the department of rehabilitation psychology and special education at the University of Wisconsin–Madison. She earned her PhD in special education from the University of Florida in 2008. Before earning her doctorate, Melinda taught in inclusive general education classrooms in the state of Florida. During this time she was also trained as an Orton Gillingham tutor and worked with adolescents with reading disabilities.